HAUNTED

TYRONE

HAUNTED
TYRONE

Cormac Strain

The
History
Press
Ireland

First published 2014

The History Press Ireland
50 City Quay
Dublin 2
Ireland
www.thehistorypress.ie

© Cormac Strain, 2014

British Library Cataloguing in Publication Data.
A catalogue record for this book is available from the British Library.

ISBN 978 1 84588 845 9

Typesetting and origination by The History Press

CONTENTS

1

BUMPS IN THE NIGHT

THERE'S a fine little village in Tyrone called Gortin (pronounced Gort-Chin), nestled snugly in the Sperrin Mountains. Not too far outside it, in the direction of Plumbridge, lies the farmhouse where our first story takes place.

In February 2012 Tim Elis, a Dubliner by birth, had travelled to the area on business. He explains what happened next:

A view of the village of Gortin.

I met my client in Omagh, which is only a handful of miles from where a college friend of mine lives. I studied with Dan McCullagh in Dublin at the turn of the century from 1998 until 2004. We were good friends and kept in touch, so after meeting my client in Omagh, I rang Dan. He gave me rough directions to his house (I say rough directions, because – to be frank – he lives in the middle of nowhere).

Dan's house is a big old farmhouse dating back to the mid-1800s – but I didn't know that at the time. All I knew was that it was getting dark and I had to get myself to a place called Gortin, where Dan would be waiting for me, and I'd follow him from there on in.

The journey itself didn't really take as long as I thought it would, and brought me through some beautiful countryside, up a mountain and

The forest park in the Gortin Glens.

cut right through a forest (the Gortin Glens Forest Park I, was later to learn) before exiting out the other side. Down the other side of the mountain I went and then, as if out of nowhere, the quaint little village of Gortin appeared. I spied Dan's car and sent him a quick text (one can never be too sure – the last thing I wanted was to end up following a complete stranger).

Satisfied it was in fact Dan, I followed the tail lights of his Honda Civic, never letting it out of my sight. When I said earlier that Dan lived in the middle of nowhere, I probably didn't stress how far into the middle of nowhere it was. In fact, it had been quite a while since I'd been there so I had forgotten just how far into the abyss we were going. Small mountainous roads lead us on and on, with rickety wire fences atop half-hidden old stone walls, eaten up by the soil and grass which seemed determined to reclaim as much as it could. Eventually we arrived. Thankfully I am a seasoned traveller of Irish roads – otherwise that experience would have put me off driving for life. I never realised roads got so narrow.

'Here we go!' said Dan, as he got out of his car and proceeded to lock it.

'Is that force of habit?' I asked. 'Surely if someone stole your car they'd either crash on those roads or be going so slow you could catch them up with a jog?'

'Ha ha,' said Dan sarcastically. 'I see your sense of humour is still terrible.'

'At least I live in an actual society,' I replied, to which Dan let out a burst of laughter.

'Ah,' he said, 'it certainly is a far cry from the city of Dublin. You won't find a clamper for miles up here.'

Dan invited me into the house, where his wife Aisling already had a fire blazing and a sturdy stew on the boil. I was starving and the smell of food just made me all the more hungry. After greeting Aisling – who, like every Irish person, just knew the right time to 'stick on' the kettle, regardless of dinner being almost ready – Dan and I engaged in small talk for a few minutes. The catching up would happen later, more than likely over a few pints.

'What do you do for a pub around here?' I asked. 'It's like you're in the middle of nowhere.'

'Ah, you know Tim,' replied Dan, 'you were always one for jumping to conclusions. Just because it's dark outside doesn't mean that there isn't a pub over the road. Granted you'll get a few stares since you aren't local, but it was one of the prerequisites before we moved here. "Find a place with a pub near it" was at the top of the list.'

That's the Dan I remembered. Always one step ahead.

'Good,' I replied. 'We've a lot to talk about, and talking makes me thirsty.'

Then it was time to tuck into the stew. Homemade stew, homemade bread and warm, sugary tea … the kind of things health fanatics might frown upon, but probably a good choice of sustenance for this kind of mountain living.

As we ate, I asked about the house – and what a house! It was big, it was old and it had a certain *je ne sais quoi* about it. I asked how Dan had managed to acquire it.

The house was big, old and had a certain je ne sais quoi *about it.*

'It was an uncle's, believe it or not. Left to me in his will, even though I had hardly ever met him. He was my godfather and considering I never saw him at my communion or confirmation, I assume he thought he'd make up for it by giving me the house. He was quite a queer fellow though. According to the family history he bought this place in the mid-1960s. Apparently he was quite an outgoing character, but he had more downs than ups in life and so he moved in here and cut himself off from everyone. In fact, when we were kids, it was rumoured amongst our other cousins that this place was haunted. Ha ha! Haunted, imagine that! That'd be a turn up for the books.'

I couldn't help but notice the quick glance that passed between husband and wife.

'I thought you said that you were looking for a place "with a pub near it"? I asked, slightly confused. As I looked to Dan for an answer, Aisling busied herself with the pot of stew.

'Some more, Tim?' she inquired, before Dan could answer my question.

As Aisling was filling my plate with more stew, Dan gave me the background history on the house – and blatantly seemed to be avoiding my question. Maybe I had caught him out. Maybe he was boasting a bit when he mentioned choosing a place near a pub, so best probably to let that line of discussion go in case it's embarrassing, I thought.

'... which is where the servants quarters were. That's been converted to a storeroom years ago though,' Dan continued, completely oblivious to my internal thinking.

Having finished our meal, I helped with the dishes before Dan suggested going for a pint. 'You two go on,' said Aisling. 'I've got some *EastEnders* to watch'. 'Be careful walking on that road at this time of night', was the last thing we heard before the front door closed and we were in the chilled night air.

There's no real need to give a detailed outline of the pub or the drinks, other than to say it was a friendly establishment where everyone really did know everyone else's name – bar mine of course. I was the stranger 'from down south'. The hours flew by and before I knew it, we were wandering back down the road to Dan's house. I hadn't actually drank very much as I was on the road the following morning. Plus, I'm not much of a drinker. Dan, on the other hand, must have drunk 6 or 7 pints and was certainly under the influence. I tried to get him to talk about the house, but all he would say to me on the way back was he hoped I got a good night's sleep though, it seemed from his expression, that might not happen. If you've ever been in that situation where you are sober and you are trying to have a conversation with a drunk person, you'll understand why I gave up trying. I just went along with what he said.

Aisling, thankfully, was still up when we got back. Dan trotted on up to his bed, leaving me standing in the hallway until Aisling came out of the kitchen, switching off the lights as she did, and gave me directions to my bedroom. It was called the Guest Room – suitably enough – and apparently had been designated as such since the house was built.

To stay on schedule, I needed to be on the road by 10 a.m. at the latest so I didn't need to be told twice where my room was. Making my way there I noticed the thick, thick walls with the deep-set widows, indicating the age of the house. As the stairs reached the third floor where my room was and I looked at the long winding corridors, I realised just how big the house was. It was massive. And cold. It was like I'd left reality behind me. There was a chill in the air and the atmosphere was almost like I was in a different building. I had to remind myself I was a grown man and not a child as I looked for the appropriate door marked 'Guest Room'.

I found it without too much delay, opened the door and immediately felt the warmth. Aisling had left the heater on so the room was very cosy. The electric blanket was also on, so at

'Find a place with a pub near it'.

least I knew I wouldn't have to worry about the chill anymore.

It was around half-past midnight by the time I was settled in bed and it probably wasn't too long afterwards that I was fast asleep. The room was comfortable, as was the bed, and it felt safe and secure so there wasn't anything keeping me awake.

Well, there wasn't anything until around 2 a.m., going by the time on my smartphone. I was woken by thumping in the walls. I say 'in the walls' because that's just what it sounded like. Groggy with sleep, I paid no heed – there was a bathroom on this floor and one on the floor below so maybe it was the pipes. The next time I awoke – well, this is what I thought at the time – it was daylight and I could smell breakfast. A good old Ulster fry up, it seemed from the smell of freshly cooked bacon. I showered, got myself ready and went downstairs.

Both Dan and Aisling were there, almost ready to tuck in. 'Ah great,' said Aisling. 'I was about to call you. Sleep well?'

'Yes,' I replied, 'though there was a bit of thumping going on, musta been around 2 a.m. Those water pipes make a bit of a racket!'

'Erm … that room is nowhere near the water pipes' said Aisling, giving Dan that same kind of glance she had the night before.

'You know what Tim?' joked Dan. 'I think you met Louis, my uncle. Did anything else happen?'

'No,' I said. 'Not that I remember.'

'Think harder,' said Tim. 'Think about it over breakfast because I have a story for you before you go.'

Eating breakfast, the strangest things were going on in my mind. I had thought I had had a full, good night's sleep, but now when I thought of it, I remembered I'd actually been woken up every hour or so. First had been the walls banging around 2 a.m. Then there were the walls banging plus two different kinds of knocking noises around 3 a.m. I remember sitting up in the bed – still half asleep – but then I fell back to sleep again. At 4 a.m. I had actually got out of bed and – low and behold – actually recorded the sounds on my phone … on video no less. I had checked every wall, trying to fathom the source of the three different sounds. But when I checked one wall for the source of the banging it sounded like it was coming from a different wall. The same thing happened when I looked for the source of the chipping sound and the tapping noises.

All this information flooded my brain. I was astounded with that I had experienced and I was even more astounded that I seemed to have forgotten about it.

'Holy c**p, Dan,' I said. 'We're going to need to talk about this'.

'I didn't want to mention it to you last night,' Dan explained, 'since not everyone who sleeps in there gets to experience it. It only happens to some people. Usually more scary than

11

your experience though. I once had a friend of mine who knocked on our bedroom door and asked if it was OK if he slept downstairs. He was hearing footsteps and everything.'

Footsteps! Another memory sprung up. 'It's just dawned on me I heard footsteps too. This sounds crazy, but I woke up to the sound of someone walking backwards and forwards between the bed and the wall. As far as I remember, I think I sat up in bed, told it to f★★k off and let me sleep, and then somehow went back to sleep again.'

'That's the same place the last fella heard someone walking. It freaked him out completely too. Now I don't know if people just forget about the incidents during the night or if they experience nothing, but one person described seeing a man and that man looked just like my uncle. I've never slept there so I've never had such an experience, but I might now, just to see what happens.'

I was only half listening. Had I told a ghost to go f★★k off? And then go back off to sleep?

No matter, it was time for me to go, time to travel back to Dublin and take this weird tale with me.

'You're more than welcome back anytime, Tim' were Dan's words to me as I left. 'Don't worry though … next time I'll put you in the other spare bedroom.'

'Yeah, next time,' I thought. I had a sneaking suspicion 'next time' wasn't going to be any time soon.

2

DREAMS OF AN OLD HAG

WE all have dreams, no matter if we remember them or not. Dreams are the mind's way of making sense of the day that's passed. Well, most of the time anyway.

Imagine if you kept having the same dream, of the same person but every dream was a continuation of the last … and each one more terrifyingly real than its predecessor. Imagine the dreams haunting you during the day and making it all the more difficult to separate imagination from reality. This is what happened to Anne McGrath of Dungannon in County Tyrone, a thirty-five-year-old mother. She recalls:

As a youth, I could probably have been described as impetuous. When I turned eighteen I had already decided I was moving out of the family home with the intention of getting a job locally and starting life.

In my mind, if I were to be an adult, then it was best to get up and do that, rather than waiting around. Shortly after my eighteenth birthday I upped sticks, said farewell to my parents and moved. OK – so I only moved a few miles away, but in the mind of eighteen-year-old me I may as well have been moving country.

I got a job at a local supermarket and moved into a flat at the top of a three-storey building with my best friend Maeve. She too had turned eighteen and had decided to be as daring as I, and move out of the family home and begin a life of her own. It's certainly not something I would encourage my own daughter to do. As I say, I was impetuous – and that's not always a good thing.

Nothing would scare me in those days. I remember Maeve and I would rent out scary movies, and it would be me who'd be laughing the whole way through whilst Maeve would be hiding behind the sofa. In the gradual change that happened my bravado disappeared.

I had a string of minor bad occurrences shortly after we had moved into the flat, and it all seemed to start after I had bought a particular painting. Meticulously painted, it depicted a bridge and the people on it, dark clouds overshadowing it. It was in itself a bit depressing looking, but that wasn't what interested me. I just thought it was really well painted and very detailed.

Maeve wasn't too happy with the painting and even went as far as doing some research on it. She found the painting was of a bridge in England where people committed suicide. I can't say it was directly linked to our bad luck, but I almost lost my job, Maeve actually did lose hers (both instances were due to pure bad luck rather than anything else) and then we ended up losing the flat itself. Before we left, Maeve threw the painting out the window. She had decided she was moving back to her parents so I was now left on my own.

I found alternative accommodation, but the place I moved to was pretty dire. I knew no one there and it was a horrible place. The rewards of impetuousness.

Though Maeve was now living at home, I still hung out with her and her friends. Maeve's friends lived in

Anne moved out of the family home to find a place of her own.

a block of flats which was almost as much of a dive as the place I lived in. Actually theirs was worse in reality. Hardly any of the lights in the building worked and there were a bunch of weirdos who lived downstairs. I'm still convinced that the strange things I experienced later were directly linked to what these people were doing.

I arrived at Maeve's friends' flat one night as I was to meet Maeve there. The whole gang of us were going out that night. The door was answered by one of the people living downstairs and as I went in I could see into their flat. It was dark and murky in there and all of them were quietly sitting on the floor in a circle, each with an arm stretched into the centre of the circle. The door closed before I could get a better look. I went upstairs to where Maeve and her friends were.

On our way back down, I asked one of the girls what the people downstairs were at. As we got to the bottom of the stairs, she knocked on the flat door, peeked in and asked, 'What are yous doing?'

'We're messing with this Ouija board,' was the reply.

I was amazed as I could see the thing their hands were on moving about. I wasn't too sure if it was doing it itself or if they were making it do it – I couldn't quite fathom the point of the exercise but it didn't really matter (at that time) too much to me. Not like now. I don't even feel comfortable saying that word 'Ouija'.

The next evening, Maeve rang me and asked had I heard what had happened the night before after we had left. I obviously hadn't. It transpired that after we had left the word 'flat' had been repeatedly spelled out. They all had assumed it meant the flat they were in. But when two of their friends, who had arrived by car, went to leave, all the tyres on their car were flat. I still didn't care. It was all bunkum anyway, just like the movies Maeve and I used to rent out. It was that night though, that the dreams started.

Well, the dreams weren't first. The first thing that happened was some form of astral projection. That night, for about five seconds, I was trying to sleep. I was looking at the fireplace off to the side of me and then the next second I was looking at myself from above, looking at the fireplace – and boom! I was back on the bed, looking at the fireplace. I was not scared then, just curious.

At that stage, emotionally I was quite messed up – something that at the time I still put down to that picture. Maeve had gone, my parents were worried about me and I was insistent I wasn't going to give in and move back home like Maeve had done. In all honesty, I wasn't happy and the future wasn't looking very bright.

The following night was when the dreams started. Weird dreams because though they were on the same theme, the content was usually

These dreams were super realistic.

slightly different. There was an old woman in it – she wasn't bent over and craggy but she seemed to be very short in stature.

In my dream she was wearing what I later found out was a hemp garment. That in itself always struck me as strange as at the time I had no idea what hemp was or what clothes made of hemp looked like. It was only with the advent of the internet that I looked it up. It was strange that I was able to dream of someone wearing a kind of cloth I had never heard of.

In this dream my whole family were in a large white car, all beckoning me to join them. Off to my left at a distance was this old woman. Initially, she was only looking at me

and I would then wake up. On following nights I had the same dream in all regards except the woman got bolder. She went from looking at me, to staring at me, to glaring at me (and each time I would wake up in a sweat) until eventually in my dream she would get closer and closer and closer. For weeks this went on until it got to the stage that I was terrified of the night. I didn't want to go to sleep.

I stopped communicating with people; I no longer hung out with Maeve or her friends. The dreams entered a new stage when the old woman started to beckon me. It was if she wanted me to follow her. There was some kind of cellar or underground tunnel which the old woman kept walking towards, all the time looking around to me, beckoning me with her finger but yet never actually saying anything. I refused to budge until eventually my dream started with me looking at the white car with my family in it, and the old woman was guiding me by the arm to the tunnel/cellar or whatever it was. That time I woke up screaming.

After about a month of these nightmares I began to think I was seeing the old woman during the day, outside the flat, at work and on the way to work. I was terrified all the time because these dreams weren't just dreams. They were becoming reality.

At this stage, I swallowed my pride, took a holiday from work and went back home for a while. I didn't tell

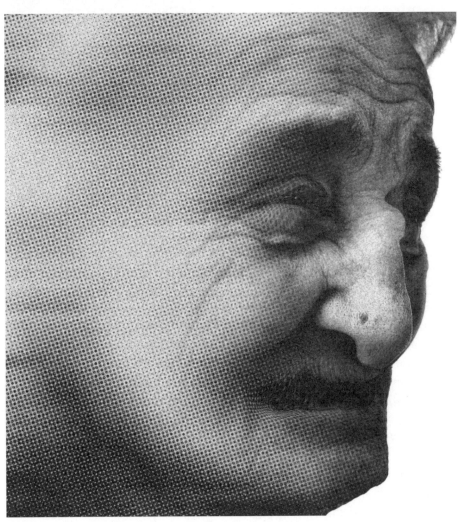

The old woman was sitting right next to Anne, staring right into her face.

my parents anything, but I'm sure they could tell that the pale, scared-looking youngster staying in their house wasn't the same person as the perky, couldn't-give-a-fig, unscarable eighteen-year-old that had left barely six months beforehand. Alas, even at home there was no hiding from the Old Hag.

This time my dream was different. I was driving along a road near to my home when I thought I saw the old woman. In fact, I thought I had run her over. In this dream I actually recognised the old woman as the Old Hag from my dreams. I was dreaming, yet I consciously recognised this woman from my other nightmares! How insane is that? These dreams were super realistic. They were of high-octane nightmare quality, super HD and not easily forgotten in the morning. In fact, not forgotten at all.

So here I am, in my dream, absolutely convinced I had run over an old woman (never mind her being the old woman I had recognised from another dream). I stopped the car, got out and searched around the front of the car, with only the headlights for illumination. No sign of anyone. I felt relieved. I opened the door of my car, got back in, turned the key and froze. The old woman was sitting right next to me, staring into my face. Once more I woke up screaming, except this time I woke the rest of the house.

That wasn't the end of it.

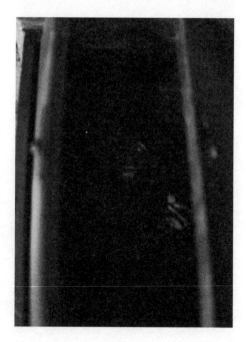

The closed door of the built-in wardrobe slowly opened.

The following night, as I lay in bed, absolutely terrified of sleeping, things cranked up a notch. The closed door of the built-in wardrobe on the other side of the room slowly opened. Inside – and I swear to this to this day – stood the old woman. For God's sake, I wasn't even asleep this time. I panicked, ran out of the room and down to the kitchen, where I switched on the TV, the radio and anything else I could find. I don't know why. I was petrified at that stage and that was when I started praying.

Up until this point I was never religious but now I had run out of options. I prayed to God, to all the saints I could think of and to the Virgin Mary and I swear that's when miracles started. I found I was brave enough to go back to my room. I realised that if I prayed myself to sleep I wouldn't have the nightmares. It was a really, really strange thing. Overnight I became uber religious and though I'm not quite that religious today, it's the main reason why I now believe in God.

I do not know where the Old Hag came from, I don't know why she chose to haunt me but I do know that I never experienced anything like it again. I personally believe something evil attached itself to me because of those people and their Ouija board and I believe it took God in all his goodness to rid me of it.

3

LADY IN A LOCKED ROOM

YOU can't have a book of Tyrone ghost stories without including Knocknamoe Castle Hotel in Omagh. A staple in the town's nightlife until it closed down, the castle was gutted by a massive fire in 1988.

As a venue, the castle played host to many famous musicians, including the late, great Rory Gallagher. During the Second World War it

US soldiers in Omagh during the Second World War.

was the US Army's headquarters and two rooms were named the Eisenhower and Montgomery Rooms to commemorate a reported meeting there between the Allied commanders prior to D-Day. Even Churchill was said to have stayed at the castle.

The castle grounds, according to some locals, were always viewed as a place of bad luck but that does not seem to be the case nowadays. Whilst researching this, I couldn't find any reports of anything untoward in the area where the castle once stood. The grounds do have a murky past though, considering a group of British Army soldiers died in a car bomb in the hotel's car park in 1973. Sporadically, over the years people have reported seeing the flash of the explosion and hearing the screams of those who died – but this is not the castle's only haunting.

As a teenager, Liam Maguire used to work part time in the hotel. He recalls:

From when I first started working there, I heard all sorts of stories about the place. I met people who swore blind that they had seen the ghostly re-enactment of the car bomb that killed British soldiers back in the early 1970s. Staff claimed to have heard all sorts of strange things in the hotel itself and witnessed objects moving on their own and various other stories. Being a big, old castle – and a big old castle with a ghostly history – you'd expect to hear these kinds of stories so they didn't faze me in the slightest. Staff said that years ago (this history seems to have been forgotten) a young lady had killed herself in an upstairs room. Her age varied – some said she was a young child, some said she was a young lady but all agreed she was young, certainly under the age of twenty.

I don't know where this information was coming from but it was water off a duck's back as far as I was concerned. Granted, there were places in the hotel where you could swear you were being watched. Places where you might be working and think another member of staff

Omagh High Street.

was there and it would end up to be nobody, but overall I was fairly sceptical about any of the stories of ghosts.

Eventually, after I'd been working there for a year or so, a co-worker and a security guard got into a conversation about the alleged ghost. The security guard recounted a few instances where he found himself chasing after people who weren't there ... he'd heard noises, sounds of something moving, gone to investigate and found nothing. My co-worker and I laughed at this, telling the security guard it was all in his mind, until he offered a wager: he would cover for us and let us into the hotel to the locked room after the nightclub had closed, if we agreed to stay in there all night. There was a crisp tenner each in it for us if we did. We'd pay him if we didn't.

'Easy money!' I thought, so then, after arranging a night to do this, my attention turned to preparation. I was still living at home, so I had to tell my parents I was staying in a friend's house on the night in question.

It was a few days before we were due to stay in the locked room, so it certainly was a few days of anxious wait. It's one thing to proclaim one's disbelief, but it's quite another to volunteer to stay in an apparently haunted room. The upside was we wouldn't be going in there until after 2 a.m., and technically it would be

morning by 6 a.m., so we only had to stay there for four hours. £2.50 an hour was a better hourly rate than I was getting paid at the time.

Eventually the day arrived. I wasn't working that night, so I actually went to the nightclub and chilled out. Afterwards, the security guard let us in and, as far as I can remember, we even managed to make ourselves a nice bit of food in the kitchen.

Eventually we made our way up the stairs to the room, the door of which was meant to have been left unlocked by the security guard. It wouldn't open. Wouldn't budge an inch. I tried to shoulder it open until I felt my shoulder would fall off, to no avail. My co-worker, McBride I think was his name, hit the door a kick but that made no difference either. We went back to find the security guard to claim our winnings, considering he hadn't kept up his side of the bargain.

'Ah, ye big chickens!' was his first remark. 'Ye's haven't even been away twenty minutes yet!'

I explained the problem with the door, to which he assured us that the door was unlocked. To prove the point he came back up with us and as soon as I tried the door, it opened with ease. We then began to splutter our apologies. 'Ah don't worry,' said the security guard. 'I heard it does that. Just make sure you don't get locked in – I hear it does that too.'

Only slightly distracted by this, we made our way into the dark room.

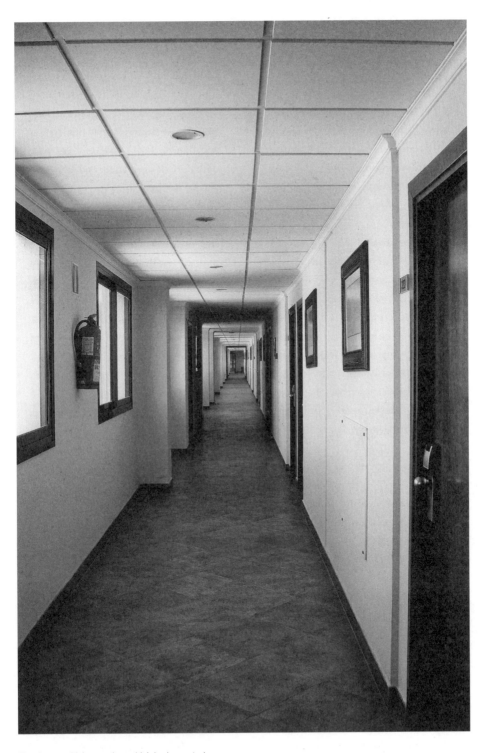

The door wouldn't open. It wouldn't budge an inch.

We didn't want to switch on the light since really this was an escapade that was strictly between the three of us and we didn't want to alert anyone else in the hotel that we were in the room. The floor we were on had no other occupants on it so we knew our door thumping probably hadn't been heard … though if it were, it may well have added to the other hotel ghost stories.

The room itself was big enough though it was virtually impossible to see much at all and I couldn't see McBride. I had sat myself down and after about ten minutes I heard noises from the other end of the room, kind of like tapping or clicking. I thought it was obviously McBride so when I heard a big dragging sound – it lasted for about three seconds – I said, 'Christ sake McBride, what the hell are you at?'

'That wasn't me,' said a voice from behind me. I spun round and I could just make out McBride sitting maybe 6 or 7 feet away from me. Then the sounds stopped.

For two fellas who went in there with big brave heads on us, we for some reason moved closer to each other. We heard things in there though, I've never heard before or since. The tapping noises were one thing but when the banging started, first we were freaked out and then we just didn't believe it. 'It has to be someone out in the corridor,' we concluded, so McBride went out the door and walked along the corridor.

Inside the room I was still hearing banging. I went to the door to call McBride back in, but would it open? The divil it would! Then I started to panic big time! I started pounding on the door, all the time trying the handle but I couldn't get out. Then the door opened, and McBride poked his head in. 'Are you alright Liam?' he asked.

With McBride once more outside the door, I closed it again and it opened without a hitch. We'd barely been in the room forty minutes, so though I was getting increasingly scared, I wasn't going to quit just yet. I took a lighter I had in my pocket and wedged it in the door jamb. I had no intention of getting stuck in this room again.

McBride came back in and for the next hour we listened to numerous rustles and bangs, which McBride could confirm were not coming from the corridor. In fact, he didn't hear any of the noises at all when he was in the corridor, yet I had heard them plainly on the far side of the room.

Curiosity began to take the place of fear. Where the hell were the sounds coming from? They were certainly emanating from inside the room, but though we had searched the dimly lit room, we couldn't find anything. Eventually we sat down at the table, intrigued and confused, but not necessarily scared. Suddenly three loud raps right from the centre of the table we were sitting at sounded. That was when we freaked out.

Imagine if I hadn't left my lighter to stop the door from closing. Imagine if we had gone to run and the door had been locked again! Thanking God for foresight, we ran in silence, out through the door and down the stairs. Only then did we start roaring at each other, 'What the hell was that?'

'Did you hear those knocks?'

'They were right beside us!'

Suddenly we remembered the alarm system. The kitchen in the hotel would have alarms set and the commotion we were making would surely set it off. We decided to get out of there before anything else happened. As soon as we got outside, who was there? Only the security guard! He'd decided to hang around just in case he had £20 to collect. We just wanted to get away from the place, which we did without too much timewasting. The security guard set the alarms, claimed his winnings and off home we went.

Now that may be the end to Liam Maguire's story, but it's not the end of the Lady in a Locked Room.

The hotel had a bit of a renovation and a face-lift and it's said that the Lady made her escape from the castle around this time. Old lore has many stories – including one that states a priest trapped the spirit in a bottle which was buried within the walls of the castle, and that during the renovations this bottle was accidently broken and the spirit escaped. People have said that a house in a nearby newly built estate is where the Lady took up residence.

Martin Quinn takes up the story:

I know for a fact that the first people to move into a certain house near Knocknamoe had some very strange experiences. I know the people concerned well, but I also know they won't talk about their experiences there.

I don't want to give names as this couple, as I say, don't wish to even talk about it to this day so it wouldn't be fair, but let's call them Tom and Anne. They were a recently married couple with a small child and when the housing estate concerned had been built they were the first people to move into this particular house. I'm not too sure when things starting happening but they didn't live in the place for more than a year before they had to move, it had got so bad.

According to Martin, the story goes as such.

Tom and Anne had just started their family and were looking for somewhere within the town to live. A new housing complex had been built not too far from Knocknamoe and they were delighted to be one of the first to move into the estate. It was a brand-spanking-new house which meant they did not have to live with the choices of previous owners, and instead got the kitchen they wanted plus were even able to have the builders customise the layout in tiny ways. They decorated the baby's room to perfection, and furnished and carpeted the house until everything was just perfect.

'I think we might have rats,' Anne said to her husband one day, when he arrived home from work.

'Rats?' said Martin. 'Are you sure? It's a new house so maybe it could be mice … I'll get some traps and lay them tomorrow.'

As good as his word, Martin got some traps and laid them throughout the house in the hopes of catching their unwanted guests.

A few days later, again at tea, Anne complained the traps didn't seem to be working. 'I don't know what it is,' she sighed when Martin pushed her on the subject, 'but during the day there's a lot of tapping noises and clicking sounds. I thought it might have been rodents, but the traps haven't caught anything.'

'It's only been a few days. Don't worry, we'll catch them.'

Later that night the couple were woken by a loud bang. It even woke the baby who started crying loudly in his room. Panicked, the concerned parents rushed in to make sure the baby hadn't fallen out of the cot, since that was what it had sounded like. Anne was first in the room. There was nothing out of place but the room was absolutely freezing.

'What happened?' asked Martin, his breath visible in the air. 'Jesus, why is it so cold in here … is the window open?' The window was open a tad, as Anne liked the idea of as much fresh air as possible. Martin closed it but he knew that it was too cold in the room to be explained by a slightly opened window. Anne picked the baby up and gave him a good cuddle until he started to doze off again. Then she put him back in the cot, wrapped him up well and once again the household went to sleep. Neither really passed any remarks on it the next day.

Over the next few months things seem to get worse. The banging noises increased, the thumping and rattling in the walls continued and never a rat or mouse was caught in the traps. As much as this confused the couple, there were no thoughts of leaving because it had been a long enough road to get to where they were presently. A few annoying sounds weren't going to drive them from their home.

However, soon it was more than sounds. At various times of the day and night, Anne and Martin noticed a mass of black that seemed to gather over the baby's cot. The priest was called and he said it must be some form of static electricity. An electrician was called. He claimed it couldn't be static electricity as going by his tests, that just didn't make sense. It was impossible for such a localised build up as the requirements for that to happen just didn't exist in that room – or the home itself. More experts and electricians were called to advise and though none ever encountered the black mass or cloud due to its sporadic nature, they all said the same thing: they couldn't find a reason for any kind of build-up of any kind to appear only above the child's cot.

Concerned for their child's safety, Martin and Anne moved out. They had been there for 7 months. Another family moved in shortly after. They lasted 3 months. Another family moved in and they too left within a short while. Then the house – itself barely a year old – was boarded up. It was just unsellable; no one would live in it.

A black cloud hung over the cot.

Rumour abounds that at some stage – this obviously can't be confirmed – the Catholic Church took the house for a period of time and after which it was unboarded and people were able to live in it again. Certainly it is lived in today so maybe the rumours were true.

Where exactly the Lady of a Locked room has gone since is anyone's guess, but she certainly could not have returned to the castle as it has been demolished.

4

THE BLACK JACKET

A small town in mid Ulster, Omagh in the 1970s boasted an array of schools of varying persuasions, including what is these days known as the South West College – though then referred to simply as 'The Tech' by locals. Accommodation in this small town

South West College in Omagh.

was limited, and sometimes students ended up in buildings that offered more than advertised – including ghosts that lived rent free. Siobhan Woods was one such student, who moved into what seemed a lovely terraced house in the town centre in a nice part of town.

Siobhan says, now twenty-five years older and still living in Omagh, recalls:

I initially lived there on my own and I loved it. It was comfortable, in a nice neighbourhood and overall I felt pretty safe and secure. I would get home from college, light the fire and get stuck into my college assignments. After a few weeks of solitude I found two other girls looking for accommodation so within a month there were three of us living in the house. We all got on brilliantly and initially we were having the time of our lives. Within another month all of this had changed.

The change happened over the course of one night. One night I and one of the girls went out for a drink. We left Teresa in the house as she wanted to catch up with some college work. We, on the other hand, decided all work and no play wasn't a good idea, so off we went. We arrived back pretty late, and noticed Teresa was still up as the lights were still on. When we got in, I had assumed we'd meet a tired Teresa who was exhausted from working on her college assignments – but instead we met an angry Teresa who didn't seem to be very happy with us.

'I suppose you think you two are so funny,' she said to us, quite sarcastically.

Long Kesh Jail, otherwise referred to as the H Blocks.

Before we go any further, I think there's a bit of history that might be important here that needs mentioning. Teresa had a boyfriend called Aiden who was at that time in Long Kesh Jail. He was a bit strange and had sent a message to Teresa telling her he was always watching, regardless of him being in jail. Looking back on it, I think her boyfriend may have been involved in some form of black magic or something of that nature.

Anyway – by this stage we were all in the kitchen and we asked Teresa what she meant.

'You know well what I mean,' she said … again, not very happy with us. 'I don't know how you knew it was

his – in fact, I didn't even know you knew about him, but you obviously thought it was funny.'

I and the other girl – Angela, I think she was called – both looked at each other and burst out laughing (we had been at the pub after all). I explained we had no clue as to what Teresa was on about. We'd gone to the pub and hadn't come back until now.

'Don't lie to me!' said Teresa. I heard you upstairs which is why I went up to look in the first place!' This sobered us up pretty quick.

'What?' both Angela and I blurted out. 'Was there someone in the house?'

Tea was made, and we all sat around the table. I explained once more to

The jacket had moved from the wardrobe to the bed.

Teresa that we hadn't been there all night, and asked her to tell us exactly what had happened.

'I was downstairs in the front room, working on my assignment, when I heard a thud from upstairs. It was like someone dropped something on the floor. I didn't think – I assumed it was you two back home so I went up to see how you had got on, and to check if everything was OK, considering I didn't hear you come in.

'When I got upstairs, there was no sign of anyone, but my bedroom door was open, as was my wardrobe. Aiden's jacket was spread out over my bed. Did you do that?'

'Teresa,' I said. 'We weren't here. Are you making this up? Because if you aren't then someone broke in …'

The three of us held hands and made our way upstairs as a group. Everything was still as Teresa had described it. Her bedroom door was open and the light was on. The wardrobe was open and there was the jacket. 'Oh shit!' screamed Teresa as she tried to run back downstairs again. 'I put that f★★king jacket away when I came up the last time!'

Now all three of us were running down the stairs and out the door. We went straight to the police station and came back up in a squad car. The two policemen checked the whole house. Not only was there no way anyone could get upstairs without coming through the downstairs, but there was no sign of any kind of forced entry. Also, the jacket was back

in the closet … even though we had all seen it on the bed before running.

After a while normality returned to the house. Either by design or by accident, Siobhan, Teresa and Angela hadn't talked about the incident and all was fine – until a few days later. Siobhan continues:

I was in my room, studying and I had assumed the other two girls were in their respective rooms doing much the same, when I heard an unmerciful scream coming from outside the door.

I rushed out, nearly ran into Angela in the hallway and we both nearly mowed down Teresa whom we found in tears, staring at the ceiling of the hallway. Access to the attic was via a small opening in the ceiling in the upstairs landing – which was where we three now were. The small access door was open, pushed to one side. None of us was tall enough to do this, and we had no ladder. We had to take Teresa into the kitchen and feed her copious amounts of tea before she calmed down.

We had initially thought we had been broken into and now thought there was definitely someone in the house. We rang around and got a few of our male friends from the course to check the house – attic and all – from top to bottom. Once again, there was no sign of anyone and no sign of forced entry. The only thing that kept me sane was the thought that Teresa was making everything up. After all, she seemed to be the central component. To me, that was the better option than either a ghost or an intruder.

Then, as they say, 'the shit got real'. Out of the three options — Teresa being mad, an intruder or a ghost — the first two were knocked off the list.

The three of us were downstairs in the front room, watching *Top of the Pops*. I can't remember what song was playing, but I do remember that it took us a few moments to realise that the banging noises we were hearing where coming from upstairs. Then it took maybe three seconds for the three of us to start panicking. It was like there was a violent party going on in Teresa's room. There was thumping, banging and dragging noises. We had started to make our

way out of the front room — to go upstairs I assume, if we had the nerve that is — when it all stopped. Just like that. One second lots of noise, next second not a thing … like we had imagined it all.

Again holding hands, the three of us crept upstairs and once more Teresa's bedroom door was open but there was no sign of the jacket or any other kind of disturbance. We weren't hanging around the house any longer. We went straight downstairs, out the door and down to the pub.

Bravado is an amazing thing, especially when fuelled by alcohol.

It must have been midnight by the time we returned, but when we did we went looking for this ghost. We were

Teresa was in the hallway, staring at the ceiling.

roaring and shouting at it until all hours, but there was no sign of it. In our drunken state we had assumed we'd told the ghost what was what and who was boss. It turned out we had only made things worse.

It was after we started hearing people talking that we got the priest in. I'd hear people talking through the walls when I knew for a fact that I was either in the house on my own or at least upstairs on my own. Then I found the other girls were experiencing the same thing. In fact, Teresa would occasionally wake up to hear someone talking in her actual room. There were numerous nights when one or all of us would wake up screaming, finding it difficult to separate dreams from reality.

The priest, though he initially seemed to brush off our tales by assuring us nothing could harm us, ended up shaking as he moved through the house, blessing it. Before leaving, he actually advised us to find alternate accommodation. We could tell he certainly did not feel comfortable in the house and didn't wish to hang around. He didn't even stay for a cup of tea.

Things got even worse then and we started to actually feel it in the air. It was palpable. The banging and thumping continued; we'd hear doors opening and closing upstairs though nothing would have changed when we'd go to check and at one stage, Teresa was physically struck by something. It had got to the stage where the three of us were sleeping in my room.

On one particular night, we were all awoken by terrible sounds from Teresa's room − a room we all knew no one was in. Then Teresa screamed and shouted 'For f**k's sake! There's no call for that Siobhan!' I had no idea what she meant. 'My God! Why did you just thump me? You thumped me in the back …'

The three of us were crammed into my single bed. I was right beside Teresa's back, so close it was physically impossible to thump her. But when we looked − there it was: a massive bruise in the shape of what looked like massive knuckles. None of us slept that night − in fact, as far as I remember the three of us just hugged each other and cried until it was daylight.

That's when I realised that I had had it. Sometimes you get to a stage when you just don't care anymore. You're scared witless, you can't run away and something just snaps inside and you decide you've had enough. That happened me and I got up, went out to the landing and started roaring at the top of my voice: 'THAT'S IT! WE'VE HAD ENOUGH! YOU CAN F**K OFF WITH YOURSELF NOW AND LEAVE US ALONE!'

Now, I swear, a gust of wind blew right past me. On the landing, inside the house. Where such a gust of wind could have come from, I don't know − but it was like someone opened a door in a gale. It lasted maybe a second.

That terrified me all over again and I lost the bravado I had just shown. I ran down the stairs with such speed that the girls upstairs though I had been thrown down the stairs – so they started screaming. I then started screaming at their screaming, which in turn made them scream even more. This self-fulfilling scream fest went on for a few minutes before the girls started calling to me, asking if I was OK. I replied I was fine, and why were they screaming?

At least we had a laugh when we realised we were all screaming for no reason.

Siobhan's brother Tom and his girlfriend were also witnesses to the goings on in the house – though they had absolutely no forewarning. Tom recalls:

Back in those days of innocence, I was barely seventeen and both I and my girlfriend had a late night out in Omagh. The only place to stay was in my sister's house. As I say, it was in the days of innocence so though my girlfriend and I shared a bed in the house, we were both fully clothed. In fact, my girlfriend actually didn't get much sleep due to my snoring.

In the early hours of the morning, I was awakened by someone opening the front door and coming in. I got up and found it was the sister of one of the other girls. She too was stuck for somewhere to stay in Omagh and as it was the weekend and the normal occupant had gone home, this particular lady was staying in her sister's room in the house. I had a quick chat and learned the girl was leaving early the next morning so she was going to sit up and watch TV. When I got back to my room, my girlfriend was awake and I told her of the late arrival. I didn't mention she was leaving early though.

At around 9 a.m. I awoke. We had breakfast etc and then left. I thought nothing more of the place until about a month later when my girlfriend and I were talking and she mentioned how she thought it weird that the girl in the house that night had stopped checking all the rooms as soon as I woke up. For a few hours beforehand, this girl had apparently been opening all the doors and closing them – even actually opening our door for a bit, before closing it again. When my girlfriend looked out into the hall to see who it was, no one was there.

However, the girl from the night before had left at 7 a.m. to catch her bus – this was something I was able to verify afterwards. We had therefore been on our own in the house for at least two hours before I had woke up. Whoever had been opening doors hadn't been human.

The mystery was never solved. Siobhan and her friends moved out of the house the following term and weren't troubled like that again. One can't help wondering that if today, in a polite, safe neighbourhood in Omagh, there is still a house that has its own, rent-free ghost that enjoys placing jackets on beds and opening and closing doors. If that's your house, be sure to let us know …

5

THE LITTLE GIRL'S HOUSE

TUCKED away in a hamlet somewhere in the parish of Cappagh in County Tyrone lies a large house, built in the mid-1800s. It's hard to tell if it is an old farmhouse or if it was built with a more business-minded aim. Over the years it has been everything from a draper's shop, to a sweet shop, to a farmhouse.

As with most old buildings, it has a varied history. This includes the premature death of a little girl who died in the house about twenty years after it was built.

The Brennan family – a large family of eight – lived in this lovely old building for many years without any talk of ghosts … mainly because Mrs Brennan kept a tight lid on any such stories. Anyone who reported anything ghostly or untoward to her was quickly told not to worry about such things and not to be spreading such rumours to other members of the family. A wise tactic when you think of the number of stories the siblings would share with each other many years later, when they had all grown, moved out and started families of their own.

'Don't get me wrong', says Darren, one of the younger family members:

The house was beautiful to live in. There wasn't a bad or scary atmosphere or anything of that nature. It was just every now and then you would hear things – and maybe, the odd time – see things.

Personally I only had a few experiences. Only one was downright scary – the others were just more intriguing. I suppose I should start with the scary one.

I was pretty young; I'd have to say somewhere around seven or eight years of age. I don't know how other young kids got on with their elder siblings but my brother Brendan, who was a couple of years older than me, was a bit of a git. One night we were both in the bedroom we shared. The light was off and we were – well at least our parents thought we were – fast asleep. We weren't though. I can't remember what I and Brendan were talking about, but for some reason the bedroom light needed to be switched on. I can't remember why but, being the youngest and easiest to manipulate, Brendan informed me that the longer the light was off, the more money it would cost our dad. At this stage I think it was somewhere around £5 million (according to the wise Brendan), so I felt I had to get up and switch the light on before the bill got any higher. I had no idea how much £5 million was, but it sounded like a lot.

So, dutifully, I got out of my bed and just as I reached the end of Brendan's bed I saw it. I still find it hard to describe what 'it' was exactly, but it froze me to the spot. I saw some kind of fiery thing, right in front of me (which was roundabouts the middle of the room), floating in mid-air. There seems to be different layers … the first outer glowing layer was bright white, inside that was some sort of bright, fiery material and then inside that there may have been a figure. I remember some kind of human semblance though I don't know if it was a face or a full figure. I was shocked at what I had seen so I didn't quite take it all in.

Some kind of fiery thing was floating in mid-air.

I screamed. I just couldn't move and couldn't stop screaming. Then it just vanished, leaving me staring at the middle of the room before I ran, panicking, to switch on the light.

What Brendan said he saw was quite different. To him, I got out of bed, walked by the bottom of his bed, then for about a second I stood there, staring, before running, screaming, to the light switch. He saw nothing. Well, I should say, 'then' he saw nothing. Years later I was to find out something different.

So, that was my first encounter and the only scary experience I ever had in the place. One thing to add to that particular experience was years, years later when I had children of my own, we were going to visit the homestead. Now I had never, ever mentioned any of these ghostly tales to my kids – in case they grew afraid of visiting their grandparents' house – but my eldest (at the time around ten or eleven) asked that we didn't stay in the same room as we had the previous time we had visited. This was the same room I had my childhood experience in. I asked him why he didn't want to stay in that room and he went on to describe to me much the same scenario I had experienced as a child. That freaked the adult me out quite a bit, but I bit my lip and assured him that he could sleep in a different room.

Back to the past. The only other experiences I had in the house were aural. The sound of a ball, marble or coin rolling was one. It always sounded like it was coming from a different room and initially I thought it was one of my brothers, dropping coins as they readied themselves for bed. This was something I only heard when younger – after I hit teenage years I don't think I ever heard it. It got to the stage though when I knew for a fact it wasn't anyone dropping coins. There were nights where I was on the only person on the top floor of the house, and I *still* heard the sounds of coins rolling. I had become so intrigued by this sound that I had started looking for the source when I heard it, but I never found anything.

Years later, I googled 'sound of marbles rolling' and it seems I'm not the only person to have heard these kinds of sounds. I have never found an explanation.

The final sound I used to hear started when I moved to an area of the house that had probably initially been some form of servants' quarters or apartment that, though attached to the main house, had in the past been accessed separately. It used to be one large old room, with high ceilings but had then been converted into two, low-ceiling bedrooms. I had one of these rooms, and boy, even though it was newly renovated and insulated, it was always, always freezing. To this day, you can walk in there and see your breath.

Outside of that, there was nothing strange about that room bar the fact that sometimes at night, when I found I couldn't sleep, I would hear breathing. Rhythmic breathing. Now I am aware you can sometimes hear yourself sleep – but on these occasions I'd be wide awake so I know it wasn't me. It also couldn't have been anyone else in that wing of the house as none were near enough for me to hear them breathing. A number of times I would sit up in bed and hear the breathing sounds coming from within the room itself.

The strange thing is that these sounds never frightened me. Instead, I found if I matched my breathing to that of the phantom one, that I'd normally drop off to sleep handily enough. Again, that's something I have never experienced since, anywhere.

After this interview I thought it wise to track down Brendan and see what his version of events was. He told me:

The funny thing is, when Darren had that experience, I saw what he was talking about, but I had promised Mum I wouldn't say a word, so I didn't. I saw that thing twice – three times if you include the dream. I'll start with the dream, as that was weird. This all happened roughly around the same time as Darren had his experience. One night, I had what can only be described as a nightmare. The dream was very realistic – the kind of one you wouldn't know was a dream at all, it was so real. It was a bit like that movie *Inception* as I had a dream I was dreaming, if you know what I mean. I thought I had

awoke from that dream, but in reality, I hadn't.

In the first dream I was in my room – the same room as Darren had his experience of an apparition. I dreamt I was looking in the mirror and I saw a face of an old woman. Then – in my dream – I woke up screaming and for some reason I got up, out of my room and went to the wing of the house that at that time was used for storage, and which later was renovated. For some reason – again this was in my dream, though I didn't realise I was dreaming at the time – I went into this storage area and there, sitting on a rocking chair, beckoning me to her, was this same old woman. I woke up screaming, but this time in reality. I screamed even more when I found myself in that very same chair in that very

This time very much awake, Brendan saw something in the mirror.

same storage area. I had somehow sleepwalked to the same place I had been dreaming about. The only thing missing was the old woman.

Besides that, I saw virtually the same as Darren did in the room, and also on another occasion when I saw it in the mirror. It was fleeting and hard to describe but I could never explain what it was or why I was seeing it. It's only now, as we've all grown older, that we've begun to talk to each other about these things and it's quite interesting the similarities between our experiences.

These two brothers weren't the only ones to experience strange things in this house. Sean, the next-door neighbour, recalls what he saw one night in the garden of the house as he passed.

I was doing odd jobs over the road for a neighbour and it was dark as I was coming home. I was walking as the job was only a few miles away and though I was tired after a hard day's work, I certainly wasn't so tired that I was hallucinating or anything, but as I walked up the last stretch of road, in the distance (maybe a quarter a mile away or less) I could see something in Brennan's garden. This was strange enough in itself as the garden was mainly surrounded by trees and it was so dark, so I shouldn't have been able to see anything.

As I got closer though, I realised it was a person. I couldn't figure it out

as it didn't look like someone with a flashlight, yet there was a faint glow around the person … enough of a glow for me to see the outline of a figure from a distance in the dark. I'm not too sure just when I realised for sure it was a person, but when I did it stopped me dead in my tracks. There was something not right here. People don't glow. I was very hesitant to go on. These were the days before mobile phones … if mobiles phones had existed I would have rang the Brennans there and then, regardless of the time and asked what was in their front garden – that's how odd this whole scenario struck me.

A girl in turn-of-the-century clothing stood in the garden.

41

I must have stood where I was for ten minutes, trying to fathom what was going on, before I told myself to pull myself together. Here I was, a grown man, afraid to walk passed my neighbour's house. Christ if anyone heard of that I'd be the laughing stock of the place, so on I continued, except now I was trying not to look into the garden.

Of course I did though and what I saw initially puzzled me, and then when it quickly dawned on me what I was looking at, I just ran. I ran and kept running until I got to my house.

I never saw this before or since and I don't even really know exactly what I was looking at but in the front garden of the house stood what looked like a young child – a girl of maybe about ten years old. She was dressed in old clothing … early 1900s type garb. She was surround in a dim kind of glow … I don't know exactly because the second I realised what I was looking at, I was gone. Away, running as fast as I could.

It is interesting to note though that three witnesses saw something 'glowing' and this may well be related to the death of that young child in the early 1900s. This little factoid though, wasn't something that anyone knew about until years later.

The two eldest brothers in the Brennan house, Joe and Seamus, also had their share of experiences, though different to those shared by their younger siblings. What Joe and Seamus experienced was a bit scarier. Joe told me:

Our room used to be right above the kitchen, and – though I can't remember the exact timing or dates – at some stage we began to hear noises. Noises from below us in the kitchen, in the dead of night, when everyone was asleep. At first we ignored it, thinking maybe Mum or Dad couldn't sleep and had gone down to the kitchen.

After a few nights of this, it began to sound like there were many people in the kitchen. We were hearing chairs scraping on the floor, dishes rattling, cutlery being move, etc. It didn't really dawn on us at the time, but the chair movements sounded like chairs on a stone floor. Our kitchen had linoleum. Chairs just wouldn't make those sounds.

Eventually, curiosity got the better of us and we had to find out what was going on. Out we went to the top of the stairs, were we sat for ten minutes or so, listening to the sounds. We were quite young and were convinced there was something happening where kids weren't invited, so we went back to bed. A few nights later the same racket began again and, being slightly braver this time, we crept down a few steps. We couldn't see any lights on downstairs and that actually frightened us a bit, so once more we retreated to our bedroom.

The sounds downstairs seemed to stop after they had reached the seventh step.

On the third occasion, we decided to go the whole hog, so down the steps we went. We got as far as maybe the seventh to last step when everything stopped. No noise, no chairs moving, no dishes rattling … nothing. Perplexed, we went back up the stairs to where we had been and it all started again. Now, don't forget, the house was pitch dark and the door from the hallway to the kitchen and scullery was closed, so we couldn't see if there was any light from the kitchen. When the sounds began again, we ventured back down, convinced now that someone was up and in the kitchen. Well, convinced a group of people were in the kitchen. This time we got to the hall door, opened it and … silence. Not only was the house silent, but also in pitch darkness. We ran back upstairs.

The next morning we confided to Mum what we had been hearing. 'Oh that's nothing,' she replied. These were the days when back doors were left unlocked so her opinion was it was tramps coming in to the house and making something to eat. She told us not to be saying anything about it. It's funny how that explanation convinced us and even though we kept hearing the noises, we never ventured downstairs again at night, convinced it really was a gang of tramps making themselves something eat. It's obvious our parents realised something was going on, but they made sure we were never frightened.

The story couldn't end until I talked to the matriarch herself, Mrs Brennan.

Of course we didn't want the children frightened, but to be honest, after I had heard the different stories from the kids I took some Holy Water and walked around every room, blessing each one. I did all the downstairs rooms and all the upstairs ones and – I swear this is the truth – as I stood at the top of the stairs, facing the front door, and as soon as I had sprinkled the very last bit of Holy Water, I heard the front door slam ferociously. The problem was, the door was already closed tightly and even though I heard the slam, I could see the door hadn't opened or closed. After that, the kids never told me of anything ghostly in the house, so who knows, maybe that was whatever it was leaving …

6

PHILLY'S PHINEST

I haven't come across too many restaurants with their own ghosts and so to find one, I went to a cosy cafe/restaurant in Omagh. This time I will not change the name nor the location, which is a rarity as I would normally, to protect anonymity. This place is so cool though; it's not somewhere you'd want to miss when travelling through Omagh.

Philly's Phinest is at 12 Bridge Street Omagh, and is undeniably 'the only Philly steak shop' in Omagh, if not Ireland itself. It is owned and run by a Philadelphian called Beth – a very nice lady who, though she still has a strong Philadelphian accent, also has a tinge of the Northern twang as well. She told me:

We moved in here about four years ago, and things were happening from the get go. In the kitchen downstairs, I was standing towards the back. On one side was a row of food baskets. It was getting dark, but I hadn't turned on all the lights as yet, and I was talking to another member of staff when one basket fell down. It startled me a little, but I didn't think it out of the ordinary and so I picked it up again. But, as soon as I had done that, a napkin literally raised itself off the counter in front of me and floated down to the ground. Then more baskets fell off the opposite counter again. I looked at the other member of staff, they looked back at me and we both started tidying up without saying a word to each other. Before this there had been various things – most of which I can't remember. There had been noises and stuff that we couldn't account for.

That does seem to be a common theme in hauntings. Many times

45

A view looking down the stairs in Philly's Phinest.

when paranormal activity first presents itself, the last thing people think of is a ghost, and therefore they ignore many of the early signs. Later on, when it becomes apparent something is going on, it's hard to recount the earliest happenings.

The second time something happened, that I can recall, was a bit more dramatic. I was cleaning the upstairs area one morning before opening. I was the only person here, and the downstairs door was locked. It was the baskets again. Normally I have them securely stacked up in the kitchen on a tabletop, and normally they stay put. This time, there I was cleaning upstairs and, over the sound of the vacuum cleaner, I heard something. I turned off the

'This is where most of the action happens,' said Beth.

vacuum and I heard what sounded like a basket falling over. When I went downstairs, every single basket was strewn over the floor. Funny thing is, I tried to replicate that and I couldn't make the same mess, unless I flung the baskets off the worktop. When I engineered a mass collapse of the baskets, they just slid on to the floor and stayed in the one area. It was then that I got a bit scared, as I realised it wasn't a matter of the baskets, for some reason, just falling off the tabletop of their own accord.

Another thing is shadows. I don't really want to think too much into this, as it's fine here with staff, or talking to you about it – but when you're on your own, the last thing you want to feel is scared … but the shadows are a bit freaky. Mainly they come from upstairs. Downstairs, it's easy to see shadows that are caused by people outside, or traffic … but it's not as easy explaining shadows on the stairs as there's no way for shadows from outside to reach there. There are also some tall people-shaped shadows upstairs but, again, those can't be coming from the outside as the upstairs windows are pretty high up and nothing would pass there to cause shadows like that.

On one occasion, two guys from the local Tech were here, doing a project on video games, and they wanted to interview me. When they got here, they set up their equipment, had everything ready to go and boom! All the batteries in all their devices went dead. They had charged them the night before, as they did before all of the interviews they had been doing. I've talked to them since, and the battery drainage only happened here and not in any of the other interviews they done.

Beth then brought me to the upstairs part of the restaurant. It fitted well with the rest of the place: comfortable, relaxing and, initially, warm. The warmth though seemed to evaporate even as we talked.

'Yeah,' said Beth as I point out the difference. 'That's pretty common up here. It can be nice and warm and then all of a sudden there will be a deep chill. Sometimes that hangs

People get the feeling they aren't alone.

about, other times, the atmosphere changes back as quick as it went cold.'

It's funny, but almost as soon as she mentioned this, the chill vanished. Beth noticed it too. 'See what I mean?'

Upstairs is a nice, fresh and comfortable-looking area. There are posters and even the odd guitar or two propped up against the wall.

'Over here, behind this wall,' continues Beth, indicating the wall furthest from the windows, 'is a storage area that I rarely use. There's a little doorway, just here,' she says, pointing at a small entranceway currently closed up with wood.

I was bringing in groceries one day for later that night. I closed the door as I came in and was walking across the shop floor to the kitchens when I heard a thunderous slam from up here. Normally you might think it had something to do with air in the building, and one door causing another door to move – but this happened after I'd closed the downstairs door and was already halfway to the kitchen. I have to admit, I freaked a bit, ran outside, locked up and didn't come back until later with a friend in toe. When we came back and checked, this door here in the storage area was wide open. It's always closed and locked, like it is now, so even if it was it slamming earlier, I don't know how as it shouldn't have been opened at all. Plus if it did slam shut, why was it open again? What seemed to have happened though – in a very illogical way – is that

The warmest day can feel icy cold in this spot.

the door slammed hard when I had come in. How it did it, I do not know.

It's interesting to note that there is a theory that ghosts will frequent areas of buildings that people don't visit often. I was starting to wonder if this was what Beth was dealing with.

There was another instance when I came up here to clean. It was after a busy lunch period and there was I and one member of staff in the building. I had come up here to clean up, as it normally gets a bit quiet in the early afternoon, leaving the other member of staff in the kitchens in case a customer came in. I was sweeping the floor, and swept from the top of the stairs over to where the little doorway is. I had bent

The area where the piano was located.

down to sweep up the bits and pieces into the dustpan and I had thought the staff member from downstairs had managed to make their way up the stairs and come up behind me, without me hearing anything because I had this definite feeling that someone had rushed right up behind me and were literally breathing down the back of my neck! I jumped up and looked around, but there was no one there. It was the same feeling you get when someone broaches your personal space. I really felt like there had been someone there – I could swear I saw a shadow and everything. It was pretty frightening. That's another thing that has never happened before or since.

The last thing I can think of is certainly one of the craziest. We were running a charity do and we had a band that was going to play to help raise some money. One of the guys from the band was up here practicing. I was downstairs, and we had the music off since the guy was upstairs playing the guitar. Now, at this stage of the day, there were only three of us in the building. Upstairs, along with the guitar, was an electric keyboard, brought by the band, but as yet not plugged in and switched off, with the volume down.

I was in the kitchens, making food and called the guitarist down to get himself something to eat. He came down the stairs, talking to me and when he got to the bottom of the stairs we hear this sound, a 'doo dee dit' from the keyboard upstairs. That was a real 'WTF?' moment. We both stared at each other, knowing that there was no one upstairs to play the keyboard plus the damn thing wasn't even plugged in. I had walked around the counter to the customer side, and the two of us sheepishly made our way upstairs, half expecting to find someone there (though how they could have walked right passed both of us without being seen would have been another question).

There was no one there, and the keyboard was still unplugged. I ran over and put my hand on the keys expecting it to make sounds, but it couldn't as it was off. Just out of sheer curiosity, I plugged it back in and was fit to make EXACTLY the same sound we had heard.

The one good thing is that there's never been anything nasty or anything bad happening, just little things. It's as if whatever's here just wants to let us know it's there.

Indeed. Maybe it just likes the smell of the mouth-watering Philly steaks Beth cooks up. Either way, Philly's Phinest can always say they have that little bit extra when it comes to hauntingly good food!

7

POLTERGEIST FARM

WE'VE all heard stories of haunted houses – usually fantastical stories with nothing credible to back them up. While researching this book, I came across one of those very same fantastical haunted-house stories ... but this one was from a group of paranormal investigators who have the video evidence to re-enforce their claims.

Cookstown High Street.

As usual with this series of Haunted books, you won't find a detailed address to the location, except to say it's in the townland of that place which boasts the longest and widest street in Northern Ireland – Cookstown, County Tyrone. Unless you know who to ask, you probably will never see the videos either. This group of paranormal researchers are just that, researchers. They aren't interested in notoriety or internet fame – they are just interested in research. In fact, posting the videos on YouTube is something to date they have avoided, considering it wouldn't help in their research at all and more than likely would end up being a distraction. I've seen the video clips though, and they are genuinely quite startling.

Robert, the spokesperson of the group who had invited me to his home to view the clips, told me:

About two years ago, we were told of a house in the area that had apparent poltergeist activity. The place is an old, abandoned farmhouse – the stereotypical 'haunted house' really – but a place, as we were to find out, that is actually haunted by something.

That really put us off at the start; the chance of somewhere having a poltergeist is rare enough as it is, never mind an old, creepy abandoned house. After a bit of research though, and after making very discreet local enquiries, we found that the house had periodically been inhabited. In fact, the current owner lived in the house for a time.

Their family moved out when the owner was a child and the place was never lived in again. It's a working farm, but the house is in pieces and is used as a storehouse. We also heard from more than one local that people avoid the place as it's meant to not just be haunted, but also be a place of bad luck.

I can only describe the owner as a very refined gentleman, a business owner whose ancestral family owned great swathes of land throughout Tyrone. Not the type for airy-fairy tales and, to be honest, after what we experienced there, I know for a fact that strange things happen in that house.

Charleville Castle.

Robert took a break to put on the kettle before continuing:

Cormac, I could say to you I'll bring you to Charleville Castle in Offaly, or Leap Castle or some other apparently haunted place … but I wouldn't guarantee you'd have a paranormal experience. I could bring you to this house and safely say there's a 95 per cent chance something paranormal would happen. That's how bad the place is. I got hit in the back twice with stones just outside the house. Wasn't sore as I had a jacket on, but I felt it alright.

The first time we went was on a Saturday evening. You only need to go into the kitchen in the house and nowhere else as the kitchen seems to be the main area of activity. As you come in the door of the kitchen and if you turn around, you'll see a shelf. I had a camera I was going to lock off and that looked like the perfect place to put it. Just as I was placing the camera on the shelf – and don't forget, this was in broad daylight and I had literally only just walked in – there was a 'WHACK' sound. Right at my feet was a large stone, spinning, as if it had flew across the room at around knee height, hit the wall and landed, just missing my toes.

There were three of us in total and the stone throwing continued within the house. It really freaked us out a bit so after five minutes or so of sporadic stone throwing, we went outside to double-check that no one

was throwing stones into the building somehow. The window panes were broken so there was always a chance of that happening.

So there we were, standing outside. Alan was leaning against the car and I and Fran were facing Alan, when the stone throwing again started … but this time, the stones were hitting the car, seemingly coming from where Fran and I were standing. That was impossible as we weren't throwing stones, and there was no one else there to throw stones, yet they were hitting the car – again around knee height – all around Alan, but not actually hitting him.

I've already mentioned there was no real need to go anywhere else in the house, but initially we had gone through the whole building and the three of us were coming back down the stairs when Fran froze on the spot and said, 'Did you hear that?'

Alan and I hadn't heard anything and said so. I had a hand-held camera with me as we walked around the house and Fran turned to me and said, 'Check that camera later. I swear I just heard a laugh.' I can't say we believed him as we stood on the stairs – but there is a laugh on the video.

At this point, Robert flicks a few switches and pulls out his camera. He found the piece of video and played it back. There is, quite clearly, a laugh and – going by the video – no one but Fran heard it. It wasn't a nice hearty laugh either. It was a short, sharp, teasing one.

'I've no idea why he heard it and we didn't … but it's obviously there,' Robert went on. 'But that was just the beginning. Stone throwing was a common occurrence anytime we went there but on one occasion there were terribly bad smells.'

Again, Robert flicks through the video recordings until he finds the one he was after. On it we see two men, both of whom were almost retching due to the horrible smell in the house. Robert on the other hand, who was behind and operating the camera, can be heard asking what the smell was, as he couldn't smell anything.

'As you can see,' Robert continues, 'Fran and Alan seem to be having trouble there. In fact, after that clip they ran outside. I couldn't smell anything and I have no problems with my sense of smell. This next clip happened when we came back inside the house again. We wanted to know if there was anyone there, so we asked.'

Again Robert flicks on the TV screen and once more we see Fran and Alan. Alan asks, 'If there's anyone here, knock on the wall.' He hadn't even finished the sentence when the camera jerks madly and Robert lets out a string of words that really should have been beeped. I looked at him quizzically.

'Just as Alan said that, something slapped me square in the back. It felt like a full, open-handed slap. You can get an idea of the force by the way both I and the camera were violently shoved forward. Again, we had to get out of the building as that scared the c★★p out of me.'

'As you might have noticed in the other clips, Fran has an EMF detector running,' Robert tells me as he pauses the video. 'Watch this …'

Robert now shows me a clip of the three of them going back inside again and as soon as they enter the kitchen, the EMF device starts to light up and beep. It does this for about forty seconds and then goes quiet. It starts and stops again and goes quiet once more.

That was the only time it did that, but there is no electricity at all in the building. As with all investigations, we leave our phones switched off in the car. We don't really understand what caused the device to go off like that.

We left shortly afterwards, but we realised there might be more to this than meets the eye and decided to make another visit, so about a week or so later we went back. Once again we started in the kitchen and we asked if there was anyone there. Nothing happened. Then we said, 'If you don't want us here let us know,' and as soon as we said that stones appeared from nowhere and bounced off the walls. We had just about recovered from this when it all happened again.

Just to prove the point, Robert played the video clip. You can hear the stones violently bouncing off the walls but there's barely enough room for the three people to stand, never mind for one of them to somehow throw stones without being caught on camera. And then there's the sheer power. The stones on the video really looked like they were fired from a catapult. That, though, wasn't what really scared the trio. Up to now, no one had been harmed. According to Robert, there were thirteen instances of stone throwing on this visit and Alan had begun to react aggressively.

> Not physically aggressive but, for example, he would say, 'I'm going to take a photo – throw a stone if you don't want me to.' Stones would then once again violently fly across the room and Alan would take a picture regardless, obviously hoping to get a photo of the stones in mid-flight.
>
> He did this maybe twice when, out of the blue, he had his tracksuit bottoms pulled right down to his ankles.

I looked at Robert saying, 'Ah, I bet you didn't get that on camera,' but to my surprise, he looked at me with a smile and said, 'Oh yes we did.' It's there on the footage and I saw it myself. You can't see all of Alan, but you can see from his shoulders to his waist, as the camera itself was on a table, pointing at the three men. It all happened as Robert has explained: the three men are in shot, Alan closest to the camera, when his trousers just disappear.

As funny as this was (I have to admit I was in stitches), the next clip showed the effect it had on Alan. He had pulled up his trousers and run outside to the car. Robert followed him out and interviewed him in the car and any thoughts I had of the whole scene being setup disappeared as I realised how absolutely terrified Alan was. The man was in total shock and he insisted the three left immediately, which they did.

They returned again … and this time it was interesting to see on video, the psychological effect the last visit had had on Alan. He wasn't wearing flimsy tracksuit bottoms anymore. Oh no. Now he had jeans with a stern leather belt and large buckle. It was just another pointer to me that this was no made-up haunting.

'Alan almost packed in paranormal research altogether – that's how badly the last incident had affected him,' Robert told me.

> It took a bit of convincing but we did all have to agree none of us had ever been physically hurt at the location. Plus, let's be honest, this is the kind of stuff paranormal researchers yearn for.
>
> We went back again and, as you'll see on the video, it was much the same thing again. Stones flying all around us – and with force as well. This time though we brought our own coloured stones, small blue ones. I was working on the assumption – still, even after all that had happened – that maybe

someone was outside in the fields, shooting stones in somehow, using a catapult or something similar. So I brought my own stones and left them in the room. If *they* were to fly around the place, then we'd know for certain the stones weren't coming from the outside.

With a flick of a switch, Robert turned on the video once more. This clip showed Robert taking out the stones – which were indeed a very bright, light shade of blue, and quite distinctive – and placing them on the little stand on the wall. Hardly a minute passed before there was the by now customary sounds of stones hitting the wall. Robert bent down with the camera, focusing on two small stones, spinning, right at his feet. They were a very bright shade of blue. He turned back to the handful of stones he had just left on the shelf – again, all of this on camera – and some of them were gone. More than two in fact, so obviously the others were somewhere else in the kitchen, on the ground.

Different-oloured stones were used, and they too flew about the room.

A house like the one at Poltergiest Farm. (© Feargal Norton, Galwayphotoblog.com)

It was at this stage that I really started to get a bit freaked out. It's grand these kind of things happening, but there's always a little voice in the back of your head saying not to worry as it's probably someone trying to fool you. I knew right then that no one was trying to fool us. We had proof positive there was something untoward going on. I was starting to get uneasy so I put the camera on the table and we all went outside for a few minutes.

I had left the camera running and we came back in, stood in front of the camera discussing what had been happening. Was it a ghost or just a series of strange occurrences? We were in the middle of debating this when, once more, Alan had his trousers pulled down again. We have that on camera as well.

He did too. Much like the last time, the three men were standing in front of the camera – Alan well buckled up. Again, in seconds, Alan was wearing only his boxers. It was like some kind of magic trick but – like all good magic tricks – it was more complicated on this occasion. Alan had a belt that was so tightly buckled that he couldn't just pull his trousers up again. He couldn't get the belt further than his knees without unbuckling it. I really expected Derren Brown or someone to appear from the shadows as this was just mad. Again there was a furore, shouting, yelling, screaming and cursing. Then, after a few seconds when I assume Alan was making himself decent, Robert grabbed the camera and the trio ran out the door.

We never went back there again after that. In fact, we haven't really talked much about the place again. It's all there on video – but I don't actually want anyone to see it. What's the point? There's something in that place and it can manipulate material things. What's saying it can't start affecting your mind as well? It's all well and good looking for ghosts, but nobody quite prepared us in what to do when you actually find one. I'm never stepping foot in that place again.

I told him I wanted to go.
    'No. Really, no. You don't. Seriously.'
    Admittedly, I haven't. As of yet anyway …

8

THE WOMAN AT THE WINDOW

NORMALLY, you would assume ghost stories are tales, passed down from generation to generation, like a family heirloom. If it gets lost or goes missing then that's it, no more ghost story.

Our next tale seems to disprove that theory, as it tells of a ghost story that the present owners of the house knew nothing about, but which fifty years beforehand was a well-known local fact.

Our story this time comes from Mr Eddie Mullen – a quiet, respectable retired farmer.

I grew up in a small townland near Castlederg and in our locality was a particular house. When I was a child – some seventy plus years ago – there was a house in our area that we all knew to be haunted. It was abandoned even then and this would have been in the thirties. Many people tried to live there, but it never seemed to work out. One of its windows was completely bricked up and came with its own selection stories and so for us kids, it was a treasure trove.

Not that any of us actually believed the stories. Granted some people tried to live there, and granted many realised they couldn't … but that didn't mean there was a ghost. There could be plenty of reasons.

Over the years, Eddie grew up, went to America and came back a self-made man. He bought himself a farm and settled down in the area and the thoughts of the old haunted house had disappeared completely from his mind.

Eddie ran his farm very efficiently and was a regular visitor to the nearest farm shop, which supplied both he and others with everything needed to run a farm business. If they didn't have what you needed, then they'd know someone who did. As with all small business, the owners and staff knew their customers well.

'I've been told, Eddie,' complained Eithne, one of the owners, 'that you knew all about Maguires' old house there outside Castlederg, and that it was haunted!'

'Maguires?' said Eddie, wracking his brain to remember. 'Maguires … whereabouts is that again? Is that near the place you bought?'

'Near it? That was the place we bought. We lost a fortune on it.'

Ah, then it all slipped into place. There was an old house, back in the day when he was growing up, that Eddie and all his cohorts used to quietly slip passed, even though it was on a hill and the road itself was way down below. They said that it was haunted by a woman: a woman who had been locked in a room many, many years before. There had been many, many stories of sightings of a woman sitting in the upstairs ruins, gazing sadly at the blocked-up window.

'You bought Maguires' house? Sure they were only ghost stories. I'm sure any old house in ruins had a ghost story. We had no TV then.' Eddie laughed off the idea of ghosts. He was

There were dragging sounds from upstairs.

more concerned though about the 'lost a fortune on it' part.

'How did you lose money? Was the structure unsafe or what happened?'

'No,' replied Eithne. 'We spend a small fortune making sure it was safe. We bought the place because we wouldn't need planning permission to fix it up, plus it came with a bit of land. At the time it seemed like a bargain.'

Eddie thought back to his recollections of the place. He and a friend who also used to walk the road below the house quite often had both had a similar experience when walking past the place – but at different times. God knows how many other people had the same experience. What had happened to Eddie was that he once looked up the hill, towards the house, to see that it was lit up, as though it was still lived in. It looked like any other house on a cold night – warm, well lit and welcoming. On a second glance though, when he realised what house he was looking at, it was once more cold, dark and quiet. It was only about a year later at a dance, when talking to a neighbour about walking passed the house on the way to the dance itself, that the neighbour made the bold claim that once he had walked the road and the house was lit up, as if someone was living there. Eddie had gone as white as a sheet.

The house was abandoned halfway through the renovations.

There was certainly something queer about the place.

'You'll have to tell me more about this,' said Eddie. 'I never put two and two together. I didn't realise it was Maguires' house you bought.'

'I'll start from the beginning,' she said. 'It'll be easier.' There wasn't a sign of joviality in Eithne's face as she began:

Tom and I wanted to find a place near Castlederg when we saw an advert for land. There was no mention of a house, just the land and a storage area. We were also looking for land, so we thought we'd give it a shot and go have a look. When we met the auctioneer, he mentioned the house and that it had been abandoned for years. It was he who put the idea of renovation into our heads, as he outlined how much money we'd have already saved if we had bought the land. Plus since there's a building there already, we wouldn't need planning permission. The auctioneer made no mention of blocked up windows or a woman trapped in a room or anything of that nature so we arranged the required money and made a start on the place.

If you go up there now, you'll see the work that was started. We fixed the walls, we put in new floors, new plumbing … all this was being done and more was planned. The place had initially looked like what it was – an old ruin of a house, with plants and small trees growing in it. By the time we had the basics done, it was as it is now … walls repaired, roofing on, flooring in and ready for the heating and new windows. We'd even taken out the blocked up window – though at that time we had no idea about its relevance or the story behind it.

Once we had got to this stage, I was obviously spending more and more time inside the house, and as more work got done, gradually I was finding myself there on my own. Tom was often with me and at the beginning, when I started to hear things, I was sure it was Tom. At the start, I didn't say anything. I'd be downstairs for example, fiddling with something or other, and I'd hear Tom upstairs. Then about thirty minutes later, he'd come in the door. I didn't ask how he managed to get downstairs and outside without me seeing him – but then I didn't see any point in asking since he obviously had been upstairs. Looking back, he hadn't though.

On another occasion, I could have sworn I had heard Tom upstairs, talking to someone on his phone. At least I thought it as him … I couldn't make out what was being said, nor actually if it was a man or woman's voice … but it had to be Tom since we were the only two there. I forgot about it after a while, engrossed in my work painting up something or other and it was only forty minutes later or so when Tom came in from the fields that I asked him how he got out without me seeing him. Tom had no idea what I was talking about. I, though, thought he was just messing so I played along and let it go.

It was only the following week when I was there on my own – and this gives me shivers just saying it – but I was downstairs, looking through a ton of brochures for the kitchen. Don't forget the house was still very much in a state. The walls were there, some electricity was in, the floors were finished but that was all. We had a small foldaway table I had been using for the painting. I was stood over this, leafing through the brochures, imaging what each individual kitchen would look like in the space we had. I heard a loud thump from upstairs. It was loud and sound like a big sack of grain falling to the floor. I thought maybe something had fallen … some of the flooring that was stacked up, or maybe some of the insulation and tools that we were readying for the attic. I went up the wooden, creaky stairs to have a look but, besides the freezing cold up there, everything was OK. I went back down to pick up where my imaginings had left off, when there was another thump … this time louder. Rats, I thought. I bet we have fecken rats up there now.

I ran up again, this time with a shovel in my hand, but once again the place was silent. Cold, but silent. I walked around, checking everything and all looked right. I couldn't work out what had fallen.

Back downstairs I went again and this time what I heard scared me.

I heard the thump, but now it was followed by a dragging noise.

I would class myself as a relatively sane person. I didn't think it was a ghost … the idea never crossed my mind. I knew it wasn't burglars since no one could get up there without passing me. What scared me was imaging how big the rat was if it was dragging stuff along the floor. I went up again, shovel very firmly ready and set to squish mode. Not a thing. I search all over and couldn't find anything out of place. I crossed the upstairs area – which was all open-plan at this stage nearly – and was making my way down the wooden staircase when I heard someone walking across the floor. I stopped and looked. The footfalls stopped too. I thought it had been my imagination so I quickly made my way down to the stairs.

As soon as I had done this, there was a terribly loud bang from upstairs and then the panicked sound of footsteps, almost falling over themselves, crossing the floor and then down the stairs. It was a massive racket, but it seemed to have stopped just short of the bottom of the stairs.

I wasn't going to go home, tell this to Tom and then tell him I didn't check to see what it was. I *had* to go look. I was scared – yet it was a lovely summer's day outside – but, mark my words, I was shaking. I went to the bottom of the stairs and looked up. I almost fainted. Hovering half-way down the staircase was a black

Some bricks still remain in the window that had been blocked up for decades.

shape. It was human shaped, maybe about 5½ feet from the ground, but the last half foot or so wasn't there. It was hovering.

I ran out backwards, afraid to face away from the shadow in case it came after me. I ran out, left the door unlocked, got in the car and drove like a maniac for fifteen minutes until I got back here to the shop.

Tom thought I had been attacked by a person, I was so shook up. I stuttered, I was stumbling about, I didn't know what to say. Tom sat me down, calmed me enough that I could say, 'You have to come back with me to the house …'

'Home?' said Tom. 'Is everything OK?'

'Not home … the new house. And no, everything is not OK!' I spluttered.

I was fit to tell him some of what happened as we drove over, but my mind was still reeling. I was having enough difficulty trying to get my head around what had happened, never mind tell Tom about it.

When we got there, everything was as it was, except my brochures were scattered all over the floor, and my little table was on its side.

Though I explained everything as best I could to Tom, all he could do was assure me all was now OK. 'It could have been birds,' he said. 'They may have got in through the new roof somewhere, and maybe that's what you saw on the stairs. Never mind that, but you're

overworked as it is. The stress of it all may just have got to you.'

I took this on board and went with it, though I decided I wasn't going to go back there for a while. It didn't end there though.

Tom had much the same experience as I had, though his was a bit more aggressive. Tom was upstairs, and kept hearing things move downstairs. It got to the stage that he secured the front door as he was convinced someone was coming in, routing through things, then making an escape once he was heard making his way downstairs.

The locked door didn't help though. At the time we had various bits and pieces for the heating downstairs … radiators and that sort of stuff. These things were being knocked over and moved about. Looking at it now, I'm convinced our renovations weren't going down very well with whatever resided in house – but at the time, Tom put it down to rodents. I'd love to see what kind of rats he imagined could knock over metal radiators.

None of this came to a head though until our son, Tommy, was over there. Tommy was student and, like most students, he was short of money. There were plenty of trees on the land and around the house – trees we wanted rid of since they were old and dangerous. Tom and I offered to pay Tommy to cut the trees down, plus he could keep whatever money he made from selling the wood. Tommy was there for maybe a day or so when he arrived home in a state, swearing he will never set foot near that house again. We asked him why – I with a sinking feeling in my stomach. 'There's a woman in the house,' he said. 'Upstairs, where the bricked up window was.'

There couldn't have been anyone as the house was locked and secured. Tommy was working outside and didn't have the keys. Tommy swears he was outside, cutting with the chainsaw, and all the while he was getting that feeling you get when you just know someone is staring at you. He looked around and there was the woman, looking out of the top window ... the one that used to be boarded up.

That was it; we washed our hands of the place. Tom uses the land and stores hay in the house. Funnily there doesn't seem to be anything going on now it's clear we aren't going to fix the house. It's also strange how it all started when we knocked in the bricked-up window.

Eithne looked at Eddie with the straightest, sternest face he'd seen. This woman wasn't joking about.

We lost a fortune on it. Still, I couldn't let it lie like that so I tried to research it. I did find that around the 1850s there was a draper living there with his wife. Respectable people it was claimed. He had a family of kids and apparently a child who had died at birth due to disabilities. A girl it was. I don't think she died at birth. I think they locked her up in that bricked-up room and now her misery haunts the place. It's a pity no one told us about this before we bought the place.

Eithne finished, giving Eddie a bit of a glare.

'Ah, now, said Eddie. 'Be fair. If anyone had warned you about ghosts you would have laughed them out of the place.'

After hearing this story from Eddie, I thought I'd go and have a look for myself. Some pictures are included with this story ... but the things I find interesting is that you can actually see some of the old bricks that had blocked up the window ... plus there's even stacks of firewood ... some cut up, and some not finished. I can't imagine anyone going to such extremes so as to make a ghost story sound better so is that the wood Tommy never finished cutting and is that the actual window where the woman may well sit to this day?

9

THE HOUSE ON
THE CORNER

THE FOLLOWING tale was told to me by Mick Malone, a native from the area of Mountfield:

When we were wee, we did odd jobs for a few bob. It was the only way to earn a few quid since you didn't get paid for helping on the farm. Not

Mowing a lawn? Sure, who's going to want a lawn mown?

Mr Fahy spent more time away from home than in the house.

that there were too many places to do odd jobs either as we were out in the sticks. I would have been, I dunno, maybe around eleven or twelve years of age and I decided during the summer months I'd branch out into lawn mowing.

'Mowing a lawn? Sure, who's going to want a lawn mown? Nearly every family around here has a load of cubs who would cut their gardens for them,' said my dad, and unfortunately he was absolutely correct.

'There's always Tom Fahy's house on the corner,' I said. Mr Fahy owned a large shop in Omagh and spent more time away from home than in the house. It was a grand size of a house too, with a few big sheds out the back and a sizeable lawn. 'I'm sure

he needs his lawn cut.' My dad gave me a strange look.

'The house on the corner? Doesn't surprise me there's never anyone home,' he said cryptically.

There was only one way to see if I could pick up some work tending the garden at Fahy's, and that was to go and ask. I waited until late in the evening so I could be sure Mr Fahy was home. His house was just up the road from mine, less than maybe half a mile, but being out in the country it was a dark road.

One advantage of having a house on a bad bend was that the council had put a light outside it, as a safety measure for motorists and pedestrians alike. People apparently had died on that corner, though not in my lifetime.

Mr Fahy was a grocer or a butcher.

Accidents had been quite frequent up until the council put the light in.

The light was a welcome sight on the dark road and I could see Mr Fahy's mustard-coloured Mercedes in the yard at the back of the house. Good. At least he was there. I'm not too sure what business Mr Fahy ran but as far as I can remember, it was either a grocery or a butcher's.

I hadn't really met Mr Fahy too much. I knew him by sight and I'm sure my father (who in my child's eyes, everyone knew) knew him to talk to – but up until then, I don't think I'd ever talked to the man. As I approached his front door, I felt very uneasy, an uneasiness I put down to the fact of having to knock on this man's door and asking for work. What if he didn't

have a lawn mower? Would I have to supply my own?

It was too late to back down now, as I had already rung the bell. There didn't seem to be any lights on and I could hear the sound of the door-bell reverberating throughout the hallway. Suddenly, light appeared along with the sound of the television, as Mr Fahy made his way from his kitchen to the front door.

'Hullo there young Mr Malone,' Mr Fahy greeted me. 'What can I do for you this evening?'

I explained my position and my desire to earn a few extra bob by looking after his garden. Surely he was too busy a man to do it himself? I couldn't see the garden in the dark, so I couldn't use it to aid me in my quest, but I did drive the point home that he could rely on me to make sure his lawn was mowed to perfection at least once a week in the summer.

'Well now,' he exclaimed, 'a man who knows what he's doing! That's what I like to see. Don't forget though, there's a garden to the side, and one at the back as well. It won't be easy work!'

I assured him that mattered not. We arranged a suitable fee with the only stipulations being that all work was to be completed before 5.30 p.m. on any day and I was not, under any circumstances, to go down the yard at the back of the house. I agreed and it was with great glee I made my way back to the house.

'If you're going to Fahy's house, take that boy McMenimum with you; I don't want you there on your own in case you hurt yourself,' said my dad. 'God forbid if you were down there on your own and had an accident or something.'

Paul McMenimum was my best friend and his family lived about a mile up the road, on the other side of the house on the corner. Personally I thought it was a bit of overkill taking Paul along – and it cut into my profits – but on the other hand there was a lot of work that needed doing, plus Paul didn't need know exactly how much I was getting paid. I decided to offer him 30 per cent of the takings, whilst pretending it was 50 per cent.

'I'll help you!' said Paul, delighted with the offer.

We had decided to start the following Monday, and continue once a week for the following few weeks. To start with all went like clockwork. We would both meet up at Mr Fahy's and go to his garden shed (which was the size of our kitchen). One of us would start the big lawnmower, while the other would take out the strimmer and we'd mow and tidy up the front garden, and then the back garden. On one occasion, during a break, we were sure we heard someone calling from down the yard, somewhere out to the far end of the back of the house. We took no notice: Mr Fahy had told me we weren't to go down there.

It was maybe a month into the summer when the first weird thing happened. We had just finished our work and had tidied up everything. OK, so we had had to break one of Mr Fahy's rules since it was 6 p.m. by the time we left, but sure, what was half an hour?

As we were doing this, we both felt the atmosphere change. The actual air itself seemed to get heavier and heavier. We were both walking out the driveway to the front of the house and, my God, I was finding I couldn't breathe. In one way I'm glad Paul was there because at least I know I wasn't imagining things, but in saying that, at the time it didn't matter because I didn't care where Paul was – I couldn't breathe and to be honest, I was struggling just to get off the driveway, on to the road and away from the house. It was the weirdest and scariest thing I had ever encountered up until then. A few yards outside the gate, it was like an invisible hand had released its grip on my throat. Paul was laying on the road, heaving. He was almost sick. I gulped air.

'What the f★★k … what the hell was that Paul? Did you get that? I nearly choked to death.'

Paul could barely talk. 'Oh my God, Mick! I couldn't breathe! What the hell just happened?'

Realising we were sitting in the middle of the road at a very bad bend, and that if we weren't careful we could unwittingly be added to the road's death toll, we both dragged ourselves back to my house, sat down by the sheds, away from everyone, and tried to uncover a logical explanation.

'It is hot today,' offered Paul. 'Maybe we had sunstroke.'

Don't forget, we're talking about a couple of eleven-year-olds here. We had no idea what sunstroke was, but it seemed to fit as an answer in our pre-teen minds. The idea that it might have been some paranormal entity hinting that it didn't want us around just didn't come into the equation.

We had convinced our child-minds that there was nothing to be concerned about, so the following week we were back at Mr Fahy's. We weren't taking any chances of finishing late this time, but try and try as we might, we could not get Mr Fahy's lawnmower to start. Not a kick out of it. We checked it for petrol, oil, tested the spark plug – but the lawnmower just sat there. We skinned knuckles pulling the start chord and were getting quite frustrated with it when Paul piped up, 'Let's run up to my house and see if we can use my dad's.'

Not wishing to waste time, and I suppose in a way more anxious than usual – considering our experience the week before – to get the job done and get out of there, we sprinted up the road to Paul's house, smuggled the lawnmower out of the shed and made our way back.

We pulled it into the front lawn, checked it had oil and petrol and I was just about to pull the cord to start it when we both heard, 'HEY YOU!', clear as day, coming from the far end of the yard. We stopped dead in our tracks. The yard led to fields, so unless someone was coming in from the fields into the yard …

Curiosity killed the cat, or so they say, and it was that self-same curiosity that now grabbed us. We stood there, intrigued more than anything else. Everywhere was silent, except for the birds and the general sound of summer.

'HEY YOU!' There it was again, still seeming to come from far down the yard. We could see no one from where we stood so both of us made a sprint for the back, stopping just as we passed the garden shed.

Suddenly there was a roar of a petroleum-powered engine as Mr Fahy's large lawnmower somehow started itself in the shed beside us. To say I nearly c★★ped myself is an understatement, but we piled into the shed, convinced Mr Fahy was in there.

There was no one, bar the lawnmower ticking over in the middle of the shed floor.

You would think your first thought would be to just get out of there – but we had heard someone calling and now someone had started the mower. There had to be someone around the place. I turned off Mr Fahy's mower and Paul and I both searched around the front and back of the house. There was no sign of anyone. It was then we decided that maybe it was best to lock everything up and come back the following morning. Something just didn't seem right.

The two of us were starting to get the inkling that things weren't all OK at Mr Fahy's. Mr Fahy himself didn't seem to spend a lot of time there during the day. I asked my dad about the place when I got home.

'I know he inherited the place from his uncle. I remember him – he was a cranky oul' git. Didn't like people being around his house, especially his orchard. Many's a time as wains we used to "raid" his apple orchard and you'd hear him yelling at you from down the yard. Died a terrible death though. Seems like he had a heart attack in the house one evening. Struggled outside and died on the driveway, gasping. I think it was one of the McMenimums that found him, or maybe it was the family that lived there before them. I have a vague recollection of it. My father always said it was a terrible thing to see a man lying dead in his driveway at 6 o'clock in the evening.'

My blood ran cold. Is that what Paul and I had experienced? Mr Fahy's uncle's death throes?

'Ah, go away out of that,' said Paul when I reported my research to him. 'You must be mad believing in ghosts.'

'Well I'm glad you don't,' I replied. We need to finish off mowing that garden so maybe you'd go and do it yourself tomorrow on your own?'

Suffice to say it was another week before either of us went back. 'We were at camp' we told Mr Fahy – which didn't quite explain the half-done job from the week before, but it seemed to work OK as an explanation nonetheless. It was good Mr Fahy didn't have kids as he'd have known schools didn't offer any kind of 'camp'. Still, he didn't ask any questions.

At this stage we'd got most of the way through the summer, but it was getting weirder and scarier every time we went back to Mr Fahy's to mow the lawns. There was something about the atmosphere of the place and I was really starting to get the feeling that we were being watched. Over the summer we realised there were all sorts of strange things going on around that house, when there'd be no one there but ourselves.

Doors would open of their own accord.

The calling from the yard continued sporadically. Nothing as dramatic as before, but we would hear voices – or more specifically, a voice, a male voice. It was usually shouting things like 'HEY YOU!' or 'GET OUT!'. Sometimes we couldn't make out what it was saying.

Then there were the things we could see happening in the house as we worked outside. The back of the house had a patio with large glass doors leading on to it. It gave us a great view into the open-plan kitchen and living area. On numerous occasions, I saw doors opening on their own and then closing again – all this whilst there was no one in the house. Paul was the first to notice this, and he thought it must be a cat or a dog – a smart animal if it could manage to not just open doors, but also close them and not be seen.

It was when I was mowing the back lawn and as I made my way up the lawn towards the back of the house, that I clearly saw the fridge door in the kitchen, open out wide and then slowly close again that I knew it wasn't a cat or a dog. No way. There was nothing there to either open or close it. We finished up as quickly as we could, tidied up and got out of there. Odd job or no odd job, there was no way I was ever going back to mow Mr Fahy's lawn again. Looking back, I've no doubt in my mind the place was haunted. Haunted, I suspect, by Mr Fahy's uncle, a man who maybe even in death doesn't want anyone on the property.

10

THE BED

THE MOST innocuous objects can sometimes cause the strangest of experiences, as was the case in the very strange story recounted by Barry McHugh and his wife Fiona. It's the story of a young couple, madly in love and just recently married and anxious to settle into their new home to journey on through life together. That was the plan anyway:

It's amazing how you can look back on parts of your life and find it all very sunny and happy. Times when everything was right, regardless of how hard you had to work or how tough life actually was in reality. That's the dream world we were living in at the time … just married, first home together and everything really was very blissful. It was lovely. We were both very happy and had spent quite a bit of time finding the most perfect place we could afford for the budget we had.

There were some downsides. We found the perfect place, but we couldn't afford to rent it furnished. It was within a ten- or fifteen-minute walk from Omagh town in a really nice housing estate. A two-storey end house, we only had a neighbour on one side and he was a very decent fellow.

The furniture we bought piece-meal – a curtain here, a table there, a few chairs. For a while we were sleeping on a mattress on the floor of the bedroom as getting a good bed was proving harder than anticipated and they were more expensive than we had thought they would be. Then we had, we thought at the time anyway, a stroke of luck.

Brian, our next-door neighbour, knocked on the door one evening. 'How are ye's? I'm Brian, I live next-door and I thought I'd just say hullo.' Funny how things like that don't happen as much these days, but this was almost thirty years ago.

We invited Brian in, stuck on the kettle for some tea and shared details of work, hobbies and whatnot. Brian worked as an engineer, travelling to various auctions every week around Tyrone. 'Any chance you could look out for a cheap enough bed for us?' I asked. That was how we managed to get ourselves a bed.

It was about ten days later or so when there was a knock on the door, and outside stood Brian with a lot of metal, held together with industrial cellophane – the kind you would see in a supermarket holding food on to a pallet. That was just the head, foot and various fixtures. He had the main part in the back of his van and, from what we could see, it was an old, old bed. It looked Victorian. The springs were the big old-fashioned kind and the head was very ornate. It was like something out of *Steptoe & Son*, the TV series from the 1960s and '70s.

'It was only a fiver,' said Brian – an amount which I gladly paid him. I couldn't help but notice Brian's limp, as he helped me bring the bed round the back so I could give it a good clean. 'What happened?' I asked him.

'I don't really know,' he said. 'It was the damnedest thing. I was putting the bed frame into the back of the van, and I thought I had it in securely but it was like it jumped sideways and caught me on the leg. I was lucky I didn't need stitches.'

Brian worked as an engineer.

'Or a Tetanus shot,' I thought. The bed was pretty grimy. It looked like whoever had it last hadn't been using it and had it stored – badly – somewhere dusty and dirty.

I assembled the bed out the back, attacked it with a stout brush and soapy water, soaked all the springs in WD40 and left the whole thing to dry out a bit in the sun. After a few more hours and a few tweaks, Fiona and I dismantled it, brought it upstairs, put it back together and threw the mattress on to it. Absolute perfection. Plus, it complemented the room nicely.

By then it was almost time to go to bed so within a couple of hours the lights were off and the house was silent. The bed was comfortable, even more comfortable considering it only cost a fiver. As I drifted off to sleep, I began to hear music. I don't know where from or anything because I was drifting off to the land of nod and, to be frank, I didn't really care. I was tired.

Over the next week, one thing I did notice was my wife's level of agitation. The least thing seemed to annoy her and, though I can hear married men reading this saying, 'That's the definition of a wife', something wasn't right. So, after choosing the right moment, I asked Fiona if everything was OK. 'Yes,' she said. 'Everything's fine.' At least I'd asked.

About a month after we had got the bed, Fiona and I seemed to be at each other's throats every five minutes. Neither of us put it down to the bed itself, but certainly our sleep was weird. I was having strange dreams and kept hearing a piece of music – it was like an old-time carnival tune, even a bit Vaudeville. I couldn't place it but when I could remember fragments of the dreams that music was playing.

I also started to become very suspicious of Fiona around that time as well. I had started hearing a man's voice around the house: I would come home from work one evening, there was no sign of Fiona and I'd heard a man's voice upstairs. I ran upstairs and found Fiona in our room, staring out the window.

'Who was that?' I demanded.

The head was very ornate.

'Who was what?' Fiona retorted, with a glare in her eyes. 'You must be going mad, hearing voices or something,' she said before storming back downstairs.

It was only a day or two later when, once again, I came home from work, but this time Fiona was sitting in her car, outside the house.

'There's somebody in there,' she whispered to me as I approached her car. 'I heard a man's voice upstairs when I came in from work. I ran out. I should have rung the police but I didn't think of it.'

These days you'd just use your mobile, but such things then were the kind of stuff you'd only see on *Star Trek*.

Man's voice? That's what I had heard. On one side of it I was relieved as obviously it was the same man I heard the other day – and therefore Fiona wasn't up to something she shouldn't have been. But on the other side of it, what man owned the voice and why (and where?) was he in our house?

'You stay put,' I said and off I went into the house. It seems illogical, but the main reason why I wasn't afraid of physically meeting someone in there was due to the last experience – when I knew I had heard a voice, but no one was there. Still though, if the owner of the voice wasn't there, where did the voice come from? That had a scare factor all of its own.

I got into the house and I have to say it seemed to have taken on a whole different vibe than usual.

I know this was just due to the circumstances themselves, but it creeped me out even more. I had to do this though. What was my other option? Sit out in the car with Fiona all night?

I searched the house high and low, in every wardrobe and cupboard, every nook and cranny. I even checked the attic and made a point of ensuring that the attic space was the way it was the last time I had been up there – self-contained and, in this instance, certainly devoid of any hiding men. The place was empty. There was no doubt about it.

Back down I went, outside to Fiona and convinced her that the place was empty. 'You must have imagined it' I said. 'How are you feeling?'

'I'm tired', she replied. 'I haven't been able to …' – Fiona's voice went on and on in the background, but I wasn't really listening to what she was saying. The way her car was parked, if you were facing the house from the street, her driver's door would be at the pavement. Fiona was sitting in the passenger seat with the windows open. I was by the passenger door, looking towards the house. I could swear I had seen someone in our bedroom, lurking just at the very limit of my field of vision.

'… just makes me very tired and edgy,' Fiona finished. I didn't let on. I didn't let on I had no idea what she had just said, nor that I thought I had seen someone in our room from where I was standing. Maybe it was just a trick of the light.

When we went back into the house, the first thing I did was check the bedroom. Looking back on it now, it's obvious that though I tried to convince myself it was a trick of the light, I didn't really believe it. Otherwise I wouldn't have checked. In fact, I managed to check the whole house (for a second time in an hour) without raising suspicion from Fiona. There was definitely no one home but us, and there was no way anyone could have got in or out without being spotted.

That night I slept even worse than normal. In fact, during the night I had what I thought was some kind of extra surrealistically real dream. It didn't dawn on me at the time to think that maybe I actually *had* been awake because really, that would have been too scary. I had dreamed there was a man in my room and he was angry with me. For whatever reason, he didn't seem to be happy that I was sleeping in his bed. Not that he could actually tell me this – he was silent. I could just tell he was angry at me.

The couple were at each other's throats every five minutes.

It was his bed, not mine – that was the vibe I was getting – and he wanted it back. The insinuation was that at present he was being nice. If he didn't get his bed back, then things just very well might take a turn for the worse.

I 'woke up' sitting upright in the bed. Last I remembered, I had been snuggled safely under the blankets.

Another few weeks went passed. Fiona was still greatly agitated but, to be honest, at that stage I really didn't care. I was knackered. I could barely drag myself out of bed in the morning to go to work, and got into the habit of catching up with my sleep on the sofa when I got home. Fiona wasn't faring much better – but again these are things you notice with hindsight. It hadn't dawned on either of us to ask the other what was wrong.

I think it was around then that we started to hear the music. It was the same kind of music I had initially heard in my dream and it was only when Fiona mentioned much the same thing that I came out of my stupor. The music was gone almost as soon as it had started, the first time we heard it we both thought it had come from outside.

'That's strange,' said Fiona. 'I had a dream that had that bit of music in it I think.'

'Jesus, so did I! How does that work out? I'm almost certain I heard that in a dream too,' I replied, 'though at the same time, I can't be sure. There wasn't much of it there.'

Indeed there hadn't. The burst of music we had heard was faint and had only lasted a handful of seconds. The thing that gets me now is how we didn't talk any more of the dream we both had had. It was like we were under some kind of spell that ensured we didn't put two and two together. From just telling you this, it's easy to see now there was something going on, but in all honesty, we didn't see that then.

Noises were next on the list. Too numerous to mention but there were bangs in the walls, clumps and thumps coming from our bedroom and various other phenomena. We thought the usual … rats, mice and even burglars, but if there had been a 'none of the above' option we would have had to choose that. We couldn't fathom it and, mixed with the fatigue, life was just becoming a depressing blur. These things had started to matter less and less to either of us.

Eventually things came to a head. I should say 'thankfully things came to a head' because Fiona and I were well on the way to splitting up, and the reason had nothing to actually do with us. Our lives were being ruined by what I can only describe as a cursed bed, but we didn't know that at that particular time. We just kept dragging on through each day as our lives lurched deeper and deeper into the dark abyss of depression. Maybe this is what the old man meant when he implied things taking a turn for the worse.

Once more it was night-time and once more I was lying in bed, asleep. I have no idea why I woke up, but one second I was fast asleep and the next I was wide awake, wide awake and completely freezing cold. From where I lay, I was staring into the darkness at the bottom of the bed. I could have sworn I had seen movement.

Alarmed, I sat bolt upright in the bed. I didn't want to turn on the light – Fiona looked distressed in her sleep and seemed almost on the verge of waking anyway. Turning on the light would just wake her up, get her angry and have me trying to explain why I was afraid of the dark.

I couldn't make anything out so I lay back down again.

As I did so, I was again looking into the blackness of the room when right in front of my eyes I saw a mist forming. It was a lightish grey colour and just seemed to materialise at the bottom of the bed. As it formed it seemed to take a shape, and just as it seemed to be forming into the shape of a man, I decided now was a damn good time to get under the blankets as much as possible. In fact, big chicken that I was, I cuddled into Fiona, hoping the apparition (which is what I had began to realise I had seen) would dissipate.

No such bloody luck. I had been lying on my back, facing the bottom of the bed, and then had turned sideways, snuggling into Fiona. I had my eyes shut but, by Jesus, I couldn't help but think someone was standing there staring at me. I opened my eyes and there, on Fiona's side of the bed, crouched over both of us, staring down, was that very same man from my dream. He was dressed in Charlie Chaplin-esq clothes and glared at us with a cold, hard stare. I must have just fainted, because as far as I remember I just fell asleep. I couldn't have just fallen asleep, not with that thing glaring like he was, so I assume the shock must have got to me because I remember no more until waking up the next morning.

It was early so it may have only been a few hours since I had fainted, but it was daylight when I awoke. There was no one there.

No old man. No grey mist.

I, though, hadn't forgotten what I'd seen. I wasn't too sure what to do. Should I wake Fiona now? Would she be angry if I did? Should I wait until she wakes? Realising that was probably the best move, I went one step further and went down to the kitchen and made us both some breakfast in bed.

Forty minutes later, Fiona was awake and pleasantly surprised with the breakfast. 'Fiona, I need to talk to you.' I said. 'What exactly have you been experiencing since we got this bed?' She looked at me out of the corner of her eye, as if not too sure what to say.

'You're going to think I'm going mad Barry,' she said. 'I think I'm going mad'.

With a bit of prompting Fiona explained how, first of all, she never slept well. She was having strange dreams and terrible nightmares which were so real. She'd dream there was a man in the room and he wasn't very happy. Much the same as, if not *exactly* the same dream I was having. My blood went cold. Fiona had even seen the grey mist turning into a 1920s man, but she was sure that was a nightmare and not real. I was certain my experience was real and not a nightmare.

'You know what?' I said. 'I want you to meet me at lunchtime. I'll wait for you outside your work. I think we need to buy a new bed.'

'I've a better idea' said Fiona. 'Let's just skip work, get rid of this bed and buy another this morning. I don't know if I can bear having this thing in the house any longer.'

We couldn't dump the bed for fear of someone else taking it home. We also obviously couldn't give it away. We'd have to destroy the thing completely. Burning it wouldn't be of any use since it was all cast iron so I rang up my mate Jim and borrowed his angle grinder. We took the bed outside and cut it into pieces. We then took the pieces, separated them into numerous bundles and dumped them in different dumps around the town environs. Whatever, or whoever, it was that obviously wouldn't let go of that bed wasn't going to harass anyone ever again.

The bed was cut to pieces with an angle grinder.

No one was ever going to have to go through the pain and mental torment it had put us through.

After the last piece had been disposed of, Fiona turned to me with the first smile I had seen on her face in months. She gave me a big sloppy kiss and said, 'Right – let's get that new bed!' She didn't need to tell me twice.

11

AND FINALLY...

NOT all stories end up long and detailed enough to fill a full chapter. Many are quite short, but yet still display all the characteristics of a classic, real-life ghost story. So, to end the book, here is a short selection of the most intriguing.

The Poltergeist Downstairs

There are many modern variations of this tale but this version comes from eighty-four-year-old Omagh man Dan Boyle and took place over seventy years ago:

I can't really remember the exact age I was at this time, but I had to be younger than eleven years old. I'm assuming I was around nine or ten. I know that because it was just before we moved into our new home

and, at the time of this occurrence, it was being renovated.

Whilst our new house was being fixed up, my parents rented a small little cottage in the same area of Omagh. Myself, my brother and my two sisters lived there, along with my parents for a lengthy period of time, but again, old age hampers my memory when it comes to the specific time period. Suffice to say this was sometime in the 1940s.

I remember this occasion not just because of what happened, but also because it was the first time I had ever seen a tomato.

We had only been living in the cottage for a few weeks when odd things began to happen. Our parents had a makeshift bed that would be assembled at night downstairs in the main room beside the fire, whilst us children all slept upstairs in what really was a bit of a gallery with a staircase than an actual upstairs with rooms. It meant we could look over the bannister down to the kitchen. The kitchen door was usually closed, and this would lead into the main room with the fire.

I was the second eldest and the youngest was my little sister, Hanna. She couldn't have been more than five years of age at this time. I remember on more than one occasion waking up because Hanna was having a full-blown conversation with nobody. The first time, I thought nothing of it and went back to sleep. The second time – which was a few nights later – I asked Hanna who she was talking to. She gave me a look as if I was stupid and said, 'I'm talking to Alan of course!' I assumed she was still asleep so, again, I thought nothing and went back to sleep. This was all days before the real scary stuff started.

After living in the house for a few weeks, myself, my sister Eileen and my elder brother Tom used to wake in the wee small hours as we'd hear someone downstairs in the kitchen. The first few times – being the well-mannered children that we were – we stayed put, assuming it was one of our parents up late for some reason. We didn't want to make a noise moving around as we would be heard, so it was best just to go back to sleep again. It was only when Hanna awoke one night and then next morning told my mother that 'Alan was cooking in the kitchen' that the conversation started about the nightly activity.

My mother brushed off 'Alan' as an imaginary friend, but got concerned when I, Tom and Eileen pointed out that we too would hear these sounds at night. 'Ah it's your imagination!' is what she would tell us, and all talk on the subject was dropped, with the distinct insinuation not to start it up again.

With no help from our parents on the issue, it was up to us to find out what was happening. That very night the three of stayed awake, waiting to see if we heard the same sounds again. We couldn't sleep since now, for the first time, we knew for certain that whatever was rattling cups, opening drawers and clashing cutlery was certainly not our parents.

After what seemed eons – and good timing too as I was almost involuntarily falling off to sleep – the sounds slowly rose from the downstairs kitchen. One thing I noticed almost right away, now I knew it wasn't a person, was that there were no sounds of footsteps or movement. It was the clinking of cups, the rattle of the knives and forks, the stretch of a drawer opening or the movement of chairs over stone. Being long before the days of portable recorders or indeed digital things like iPhones, there was no way we could record any of this and therefor no way of verifying anything afterwards – but Eileen, Tom and I sat up in bed wide-eyed, listening to these sounds. I don't think we were afraid to begin with because we knew it was downstairs – not upstairs, where we were.

'What will we do?' whispered Tom.

'What *can* we do?' Eileen replied. The situation may have been catching up with her because, though she seemed quite calm, the pitch of her whisper seemed to suggest she was becoming more aware of the horror.

'One of us needs to go look,' I said. 'It's only over there to the bannister.'

'You!' said Tom and Eileen almost in unison. 'If it's "only" over there,' Tom continued, 'then off you go!'

It's funny the things a younger brother will do when it comes to bragging rights over an elder brother. What was the worse thing that could happen anyway? All I had to do was get out of bed, get on my belly and crawl the few feet to the bannister where I could peek down into the kitchen.

'OK then, I will!' I replied. 'I'm not a big chicken like you!'

With that final dramatic whisper, I got on to the floor – amidst the banging and crashing downstairs – crawled over the banister and peeked down.

Not only was nothing moving or anything changed, but that instant the noises stopped. I didn't know what to think. Had it stopped because whatever it was had gone away? Or was it now watching me, trying to figure out my next move? This last thought caused me to scream, and since Eileen and Tom could only see that I had looked over the bannister and

started screaming, they also began screaming. This in turn woke up Hanna – who also joined in – until finally my parents ran up to us and calmed us all down. Eileen, Tom and I told our story and Hanna piped up saying, 'But I told you already – that's Alan!'

None of us had any idea who this Alan person was, including Hanna. She was of the age when it didn't seem strange that someone outside the family seemed to be in the house. Hanna was completely comfortable with whoever 'Alan' was.

The rest of us kids weren't and we were eventually convinced by our parents that the sounds must have been a mouse. The fact the 'mouse' only seemed to run about at night and that there didn't seem to be any sign of it at all during the day (plus when did a mouse ever open and close drawers?) were things we didn't think about but by the time we had left that house, we were all accustomed to the nightly sounds which seemed – and again this could be just my memory – to occur every single night afterwards. I never found out the cause and as far as I know, that little cottage has long been demolished.

Strange Encounters in the Graveyard

'People think you're mad when you tell them these things,' says Sean Maguire as he pours me a cup of tea.

We're in the townland of Mountjoy, just outside Omagh. Sean has had a couple of different experiences at a nearby rural church and graveyard:

I know there are people in this area who probably think I'm crackers – mainly because of the experiences I've had. On one occasion, I was in the graveyard with a friend of mine. The paths are narrow so we were walking side by side when suddenly both of us were pushed aside. It was like something of great force had rushed along the path and ran in between both of us. I nearly landed in the graveside next to me it was that strong of a push. I wasn't on my own that time, so there was a witness but besides the shock of it, there was nothing else. There were no scary feelings before or after – it was just that it happened so quick, and was so forceful, that we were both in shock for a while after. It never happened before or since.

I asked Sean if he had seen anything 'paranormal' at the time:

Nothing. I just felt the force of it. Imagine someone shoving their way in between two people – that's what it was like. There have been a few times I've seen things all the same, and one of them at that very same church. Once I was coming out of the graveyard and making my way to the main gates when I noticed, standing on the other side of the gate and initially hidden by the high wall, was a man. Two things were strange about him

Sean Maguire had a strange encounter near Mountjoy.

though. First off, he seemed to be a different hue of colour. It's hard to describe, but he didn't seem to be the same colour tone as his surroundings. Secondly, he was dressed like a gentleman from the 1800s. As I walked towards the gate, I caught a glimpse of him three times – each time broken as he went from view behind the wall. By the time I got to the gate and looked around the wall, there was no one there. I got in the car and drove up and down the road searching – there was no sign of anyone, never mind a man in nineteenth-century clothes who seemed to be a different hue from his surroundings. I think it was this man …

Sean produces an old sketching of a gentleman in nineteenth-century garb. The location of the sketch is roughly the same location in which Sean had his experience.

'Obviously I have no idea if it is the same person, but it's from the same area.'

Personally I didn't doubt Sean's story – but the sketch could have been of anyone. It's an intriguing story nonetheless.

The Man with the Beard

Another story, again from the Omagh area, comes from a man called Tom McCullagh:

About ten years back my brother passed away from cancer. He was living in Germany at the time and the family here in Ireland didn't actually know of his death.

My sister had two children and on the night of our brother's death, she had put the kids to bed and, it being the summer and still daylight, it normally took the children half an hour to settle down. On this particular night they were exceptionally active, taking much longer to settle than normal. My sister went up to them three times, and on the fourth time she decided to sit down and tell them a story in the hopes of getting them to nod off to sleep.

As she was telling a story, both children were acting strangely, in that they kept giggling and laughing and giving each other secretive glances until my sister slapped the book closed and asked just what was going on. Now both children were young – the eldest probably no more than eight years of age – and in response to their mother, both pointed behind her and said, 'But the man with the beard is making funny faces.'

My sister spun around. There was obviously no one there.

'Ah, don't be trying to fool me!' she said, though at the same time frightened enough to swing round to look behind herself again. 'Never mind the man with the beard and settle down,' she continued.

As it happened the kids settled and went off to sleep and my sister had no idea whom it was the kids had seen.

The next morning news of our brother's death arrived, and it was only at the wake that the youngest went into hysterics. Then so did the second child and both ran out of the house into the back garden. My sister, worried, hurried out after them to console both children. As she hugged them the youngest sobbed, 'That's the man with the beard who was making funny faces.'

The blood in my sister's veins froze. She showed the kids some photos of our brother and they were adamant that he was the man who had been in their room entertaining them, on the very night that he had died in a different country.

ABOUT THE AUTHOR

CORMAC STRAIN first became interested in the paranormal when, as a seventeen-year-old student in Derry, he and his housemates found themselves living with a poltergeist.

In 2004 Cormac founded the Leinster Paranormal Research Society. Although based in Carlow, the society runs regular investigations into paranormal activity throughout Ireland and Northern Ireland. More information can be found on their website, www.leinsterparanormal.com.

Cormac's first book, written with fellow paranormal researcher Danny Carthy, *Haunted Carlow*, was published in 2011 and *Haunted Kilkenny* was published the following year.

Also from The History Press

A SPOOKY SELECTION

Also from The History Press

We are proud to present our historical crime fiction imprint, The Mystery Press, featuring a dynamic and growing list of titles written by diverse and respected authors, united by the distinctiveness and excellence of their writing. From a collection of thrilling tales by the CWA Short Story Dagger award-winning Murder Squad, to a Victorian lady detective determined to solve some sinister cases of murder in London, these books will appeal to serious crime fiction enthusiasts as well as those who simply fancy a rousing read.

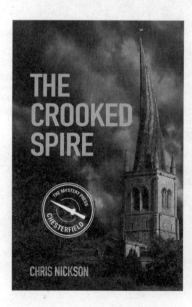

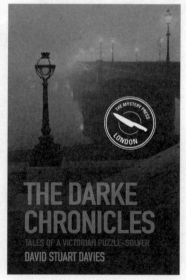